THE NEW ORU

EMPOWERED FOR THE
21ST CENTURY

NEIL ESKELIN

The New ORU

Copyright 2018 by Oral Roberts University.

ISBN: 978-0-692-99685-0

Published by

ORAL ROBERTS UNIVERSITY
7777 SOUTH LEWIS AVENUE
TULSA, OKLAHOMA 74171

DEDICATION

*This book is dedicated to the past
and present faculty and staff of ORU.
Although your contributions may have been
behind the scenes and often unrecognized,
your deep commitment and diligent work
during the past half-century have played a
significant part in making Oral Roberts
University what it is today.*

CONTENTS

INTRODUCTION

You are about to read the remarkable story of a university that was headed for bankruptcy and about to close its doors.

In 1960, evangelist Oral Roberts had a vision to build an academic institution in Tulsa, Oklahoma, to train young men and women in what he called a "Whole Person" education —intellectually, socially, physically, professionally, and spiritually. Five years later, on a stunning new campus with seven futuristic buildings, just over 300 students arrived. The student body may have been small, but their thoughts certainly weren't. They believed Roberts when he told them again and again, "Make no little plans here."

As you will discover on these pages, Oral Roberts University grew at a breathtaking pace, but the cost of major expansion resulted in escalating debt and an inability to pay for deferred maintenance of its buildings. This, combined with administrative issues and decreasing enrollment, sent the university into what many called "a downward death spiral." Its very survival was at stake.

Roberts's autobiography, published in 1995, was titled *Expect A Miracle*—and one was certainly needed.

As a result of some unexpected circumstances, ORU was

given a financial lifeline. However, as you will read, the university needed far more than money; it needed economic accountability, a new Board of Trustees, fresh leadership, and a new system of governance.

You will be taken behind the scenes and learn how the specific actions and responsibilities of the new board, revised university bylaws, a commitment to shared governance, and presidential leadership resulted in a dramatic turnaround. In a surprisingly short time, existing buildings on campus were updated and reimagined for today's student and tomorrow's world. Most importantly, the vision of the founder—even after his death—never wavered.

While having lunch with Pat Robertson at a restaurant in Richmond, Virginia, in the summer of 1960, Oral Roberts wrote on a napkin the words God had spoken to him:

> *Raise up your students to hear My voice,*
> *   to go where My light is dim,*
> *Where My voice is small and My healing power*
> *   is not known.*
> *To go even to the uttermost bounds of the earth.*
> *Their work will exceed yours*
> *   And in this I am well pleased.*

This book contains valuable lessons for leaders of both

public and private universities—especially regarding vision, purpose, finances, and governance.

It should also be required reading for any person connected to the university:

- ORU students, prospective students, and their parents will have an insight into the unique history, purpose, and future of the university.
- Faculty, staff, and administrators will gain a deeper appreciation for the roles they now play in ORU's governance.
- Alumni will gain an understanding of the trials their alma mater has gone through, and why they can take immense pride in the global university it has become.
- Donors of the past and present will take satisfaction that their financial seeds, whether large or small, have been planted in good soil.

The deep roots of the university's past have given it the strength and ability to grow and blossom in this exciting season—and for the years ahead.

This is *The New ORU.*

1

A CAMPUS IN CRISIS

It was October, 2007.

If you lived in Oklahoma, it was almost impossible to miss the daily media accounts that shed a negative light on one of the region's premier educational institutions, Oral Roberts University.

On the front pages of the *Tulsa World* and the *Oklahoman* were headlines that read, "Three Former ORU Faculty Sue for Wrongful Termination," "ORU Professors Vote 'No Confidence' in Richard Roberts," and "President of Oral Roberts University Takes Leave of Absence."

In Oklahoma City, a successful businessman, David Green, founder of the national arts and crafts chain, Hobby Lobby, took notice of the stories. What really sparked his attention was an article, "ORU Review Targeting Finances." It was a report by accreditation officials of the Higher Learning Commission detailing that the university was more than $50 million in debt. This wasn't hearsay or the complaints of a disgruntled employee. The school was being given failing grades on leadership, governance, and finances —rather serious matters.

Rumors were circulating that ORU may have to close its doors, and this began to trouble Green. As he recalls, "When I read the news stories of what was happening to a Christian university, somehow, the Lord caused me to grieve over the situation. I couldn't erase it from my mind."

Green never attended college but, being raised in a Pentecostal tradition, had followed the ministry of evangelist Oral Roberts and was aware of ORU. However, he didn't know anybody on the campus.

David Green called his family together and told them, "We need to pray about this." And they did.

At almost this exact time, David's son Mart Green visited the ORU campus. It had nothing to do with his father's concern of the impending collapse of the university. Rather, his daughter, Amy, was a senior in high school and when asked what college she was thinking about attending, she replied, "ORU."

The only other time Mart and his family had stepped foot on campus was for a Bill Gaither Gospel music concert at the Mabee Center. So he and his wife, Diana, drove Amy over for an official visit.

Mart remembers, "The admissions office arranged to have Amy spend the night in a girls' dorm with a student. But on arrival, we learned they had double-assigned prospective students and they placed her in another dorm. She came running out to our car, saying, 'I don't like it here.'"

Amy had no idea Mart was looking at ORU for any other reason—and his wife later asked him, "Why would you get involved with a school our daughter doesn't like?" Mart was concerned too, wondering if it was wise for Amy to attend a university embroiled in so many problems.

At a parents' meeting during the visit, Billy Joe Daugherty, who assumed administrative leadership while Richard Roberts was on a temporary leave of absence, opened the floor to questions—and there were many. Mart had to give him kudos for facing the university's troubles head-on.

The next spring, when her close friend made the decision to attend ORU, Amy enrolled, too.

AN EMERGENCY MEETING

The leadership and financial crisis grew so serious that Oral Roberts flew from his home in Southern California to Tulsa. In response to the "no confidence" vote by the faculty, Oral called an "emergency meeting" in an attempt to persuade them to rescind their vote and have Richard, his son, reinstated from temporarily stepping down as president.

Richard had been president since 1993, the year 75-year-old Oral retired and he and his wife, Evelyn, moved to

Southern California. Evelyn passed away in 2005.

As reported in the *Oklahoman,* November 15, 2007, "Toward the end of the hours-long meeting...Oral Roberts asked the faculty who were willing to forgive and start fresh to stand up."

It was obvious that the faculty was not ready to reverse their vote. Provost Mark Lewandowski let it be known that he would resign if Roberts was allowed to return.

On Friday, November 23, the day after Thanksgiving, Richard Roberts made it official. In his resignation letter to the Board of Regents, he wrote, "I love ORU with all my heart. I love the students, faculty, staff, and administration and I want to see God's best for all of them."

Three days later, the Board was scheduled to meet and it was announced that Regent Billy Joe Daugherty would continue to assume administrative responsibilities of the office of president, working together with Chancellor Oral Roberts until the Regents meeting.

In Oklahoma City, the news really hit David Green hard. As he recalls, "On Saturday morning, my son, Mart, called me and said, 'I think we ought to let ORU know that we are praying about getting involved.'"

He asked Mart, "Do you know anyone to call?"

Mart knew in his heart that God was at work in this situation. Starting in 1998, Mart made a vow to the Lord that he would go on an annual fast beginning 40 days before Thanksgiving, and he had faithfully honored that promise for the previous ten years. As he describes it, "I told God I would only break the fast if I became hungry. The first year, it lasted the full 40 days, but in other years it was 15, 20, or 30. However, *this* pre-Thanksgiving fast continued the full 40 days and I knew the Lord was about to perform something special."

Mart had met Billy Joe Daugherty some years earlier and was able to reach him by phone. After a few pleasantries, Mart Green came right to the point: "If we wanted to help ORU, what would be the process?"

Daugherty didn't hesitate with an answer: "Our Board meets in three days and we need you here on Tuesday!"

When Mart asked him about the financial pressures they were facing, he learned it was much more than the $50 million that had been reported.

STRINGS ATTACHED

Mart phoned his dad and brother, Steve, and they agreed to hold a family board meeting at the Hobby Lobby offices after church that Sunday. As the Greens sat around the table, David said, "We've never done anything like this before. We have never given to an organization and asked them to make changes."

Hobby Lobby has made a habit of not blessing what God doesn't bless. In other words, they don't financially support an organization or a cause unless they believe that going forward it would succeed. Now they were contemplating undergirding an institution they felt lacked the right leadership and was financially in deep trouble.

At that meeting, they wrote up a short proposal, ready to present to the ORU Board.

As David Green expresses it, "You can't live without a brain, and you can't have a brain without a heart—it takes both. And it takes both leadership and finances to succeed."

On Monday, David and his two sons, Mart and Steve, drove to Tulsa. In a preliminary meeting, they reviewed the list of members of the ORU Board of Regents, many of whom were high-profile ministers including television evangelists Kenneth Copeland, Benny Hinn, Creflo Dollar, Jesse Duplantis, Marilyn Hickey, and John Hagee. Chairman of the board was George Pearsons (son-in-law of Kenneth Copeland and pastor of a church in Newark, Texas).

At the time, the university had 23 Business Regents and 18 others who were either Spiritual Regents, Associate Regents, or Regents Emeritus. According to ORU's bylaws, those 18 did not have a vote in business and financial matters, nor did the Business Regents have any say regarding spritual matters. The bylaws, as amended April 27, 2004, specifically stated (Article 2:3): "The Board of Regents shall be divided into two separate boards of regents. The Board of Business Regents and the Board of Spiritual Regents. In the event a decision of the Spiritual Regents is in conflict with a decision by the Business Regents, on any purely spiritual matter within the purview of the Spiritual Regents, the decision of the Board of Spiritual Regents shall prevail."

It had become clear that since its inception, the university functioned under a bureaucratic governance system, consisting of hierarchies of the supervisory line-staff relationship called vertical or authoritarian governance. The tradition of a predominate Presidential-style leadership remained strong throughout the years. Eventually, however, this type of governance system was no longer effective at ORU, causing the near-demise and dissolution of the university.

Enrollment was declining, debt was becoming insurmountable, and after years of deferred maintenance, the campus buildings were in dire need of repair and updating.

In the opinion of outside observers, the bylaws of ORU had become obsolete and were not adequate to govern this present-day university.

The position of the Green family was clear. They would help the school if there were major changes in governance.

At the Board meeting, David Green presented the

proposal—to give ORU $70 million. This was more than they had ever given to any cause or organization. The school would receive $8 million immediately, and the remaining $62 million when the changes in board members, leadership, and government were approved and official. The money was to be used to help reduce the university's debt and its deferred maintenance. In return, however, there would have to be a major reorganization of the school's leadership and financial accountability.

If not, the $8 million would have to be refunded.

Red flags were raised immediately. "We can't do that," responded the school's financial officer. "We are not allowed to sign anything. The banks won't let us borrow another dime."

So the Greens conferred, then replied, "We feel God is leading us, and this is something we are supposed to do." So they donated the $8 million with no strings attached.

NOW THE HARD PART

The Board of Regents accepted the Green family's initial gift enthusiastically, even though there were countless urgent issues in the days ahead—and before the next scheduled board meeting in January, 2008.

David Green put Mart in charge of spearheading this

enormous challenge, and he certainly was prepared. In addition to being Board Chair of Hobby Lobby, Mart had a long history of involvement in enterprises. At 19, he established Mardel, a large chain of Christian and educational supply stores. He later founded Bearing Fruit Communications, producing award-winning documentaries including *Beyond the Gates of Splendor.* And in 2002, Mart launched Every Tribe Entertainment, a full feature film production company that released *End of the Spear* and other motion pictures shown in major theaters across the nation.

Mart came to ORU with a strong business sense and a passion to impact the culture spiritually. But now he was embarking on a steep learning curve regarding university governance.

When he asked friends and associates who could advise him, one name repeatedly kept rising to the forefront: Dr. Robert E. Cooley, President Emeritus of Gordon-Conwell Theological Seminary in South Hamilton, Massachusetts. Since Cooley was the son of an Assemblies of God minister, he had a rich heritage in Pentecostal tradition. He was a sought-after authority on theological school governance and board development—and past president of the Association of Theological Schools (ATS).

Along with some advisors (including a finance expert, a public relations officer, and Mart's brother, Steve), they flew to Charlotte, North Carolina, on December 4, 2007, for a two-day meeting with Cooley. It was there they were introduced to the concept of shared governance.

During the next three weeks, Cooley and Green's team pieced together a proposal for the January Board of Regents meeting. It was an honest analysis of ORU's situation and included a specific prescription for change.

The document spelled out that the Oral Roberts Evangelistic Association and the university would need to become totally separate entities. Also, the Board of Regents would be eliminated and replaced by a new Board of Trustees with eventually as many as 33 members. The new trustees would have four major responsibilities:

1. To safeguard ORU's mission
2. To select and support the president
3. To provide adequate financial resources for the university
4. To establish policies and planning through the process of shared governance

The proposal also called for a new advisory board. The former Board of Regents would be given an invitation to join a "Board of Reference."

Regarding financial transparency, the university would

seek full membership in the highly respected Evangelical Council of Financial Accountability.

Pertaining to the major gift from the Green Family, the trustees would have sole control.

DECISION DAY

January 14, 2008, was a red-letter day. Mart Green was joined by his father, David, along with Robert Cooley, and the Green family attorney and accountant to meet with ORU's Board of Regents.

On the front row sat Oral and Richard Roberts. Seated next to them were John Hagee, Marilyn Hickey, and Kenneth Copeland, along with business and spiritual regents.

Following the Green proposal, Cooley spoke on shared governance, then introduced Robert Landrebe, the Chief Financial Officer of Gordon-Conwell Theological Seminary who gave a PowerPoint presentation, a realistic assessment of ORU's financial picture which detailed why the school was on the brink of bankruptcy.

After a question-and-answer period, Oral stood up and began to speak. For nearly one hour, the founder of the school spoke from his heart about his vision for ORU and how difficult it was to reach this moment in time.

The Greens and other guests then left the room, allowing

the board to make the most important decision in the history of the university.

If the Regents refused the terms offered, the Greens were fully prepared to walk away.

2

"BUILD ME A UNIVERSITY"

The traffic jam in Tulsa was horrendous. On Sunday afternoon, April 2, 1967, more than 18,000 people were trying to reach what used to be alfalfa farmland at 77th and South Lewis Avenue. But now, on that same property, were several new gleaming buildings with futuristic architecture. The official dedication of Oral Roberts University was about to commence.

Seated on an outdoor platform were dignitaries from business, government, education, and religion—including U.S. senators and the governor of Oklahoma. Official delegates from 120 of the leading colleges and universities across the country were part of the ceremony, but most had come to hear the dedication address from none other than Billy Graham.

In the religious world, this was symbolic, especially since the most prominent evangelical evangelist would give his blessing on an institution that had risen from Pentecostal roots.

Behind the raised platform stood a blue column with the initials ORU and the words, "Mind, Body, Spirit." There was also the slogan, "Education for the Whole Man."

In his memorable 30-minute address, Graham used the occasion to state how far our educational institutions had drifted from their founding. Specifically, he stated, "On June 3, 1752, when Columbia University was established, its founders put down as their chief task, 'to teach young people to know God and Jesus Christ and to serve them with a perfect heart and a willing mind.'"

Then Billy Graham made this bold statement: "If God has ordained this university, it will be blessed, and if not, it will be cursed."

HUMBLE ROOTS

Perhaps the proudest person in attendance that day was Claudius Roberts, Oral's elderly mother (his father had recently passed away).

She could remember the time in Ada, Oklahoma, when her 17-year-old son was bedridden for five months with tuberculosis. His weight had plummeted to 120 pounds and, for his height, he was practically a skeleton.

Oral's parents, Ellis and Claudius, were strong Christians and faithfully prayed for him every day. They couldn't understand why God did not heal their son, especially since, while his mother was pregnant, she committed him to God's service.

The Roberts family was extremely poor, and when Oral reached the age of 16, he moved away from home, dreaming of a better life. At the same time he turned his back on God and began living a rather wild life. And that's when his health collapsed.

The Lord spoke to Oral's older sister, Jewel, and let her know that her brother was going to be healed. About the same time, Oral gave his life to Christ.

A traveling healing evangelist, George Moncey, came to Ada, pitched a tent, and Oral's brother, Elmer, decided to bring him to one of the meetings. On the way to the tent, God clearly spoke to Oral, saying, "Son, I am going to heal you and you are to take My healing power to your generation. You are to build Me a university and build it on My authority and on the Holy Spirit."

In the meeting, Oral was too weak to walk to the front for prayer—and had to wait for the evangelist to come to him. It was 11 o'clock at night before Moncey laid hands on Oral and anointed him with oil. As Roberts recalled, "The power of God washed over me and I was instantly healed." Not only did the tuberculosis disappear, but Oral, who suffered from a severe stuttering problem, discovered that was gone too!

Roberts was ordained by the Pentecostal Holiness church in 1936, and was soon an outstanding minister of the denomination. He also enrolled at Phillips University in Enid, Oklahoma, and at Oklahoma Baptist University in Shawnee. During the next few years he pastored four PH churches with his new bride, Evelyn.

HEALING WATERS

In 1947, the Lord strongly impressed Oral to get down on his knees and read the four Gospels and the book of Acts three times consecutively. This was when God began to reveal Jesus as the healer as never before. Also, reading 3 John 2, Oral became convinced that the Lord wants people to be whole in every area of their lives, beginning with their souls.

Oral started holding special healing meetings in his town and miracles began to multiply. When a deranged man tried to shoot him, the national media picked up the story and people flocked to his meetings as never before.

On faith, he resigned as pastor and purchased a tent that seated 2,000. Soon, it wasn't big enough to hold the crowds, so he found one that held 12,500 and launched the Oral Roberts Evangelistic Association.

Within months, his *Healing Waters* magazine was being

published, and films of his crusades became a weekly television program.

The monthly magazine was renamed *Abundant Life* in 1956, and eventually reached a circulation of over one million. His monthly column appeared in over 600 newspapers, and by 1980, more than 15 million of his 88 books had been sold.

Roberts loved to preach. Even though he never attended seminary, his messages were not only biblical, but memorable, especially his sermon, "The Fourth Man."

Millions gave their lives to Christ through his ministry, and he personally laid hands on and prayed for over one million people.

An aspect of his crusades that many overlook is that during the 1950s, when America was racially divided, Oral was colorblind and his altar calls were integrated. After an incident in one of his tent revivals, he refused to hold future meetings where segregated seating was enforced.

THE COMMISSION

In the summer of 1960, Oral Roberts experienced what obviously became a major turning point in his life and ministry. He heard what he referred to as a "commission" or a mandate from God Himself, saying, "Raise up your students to hear My voice, to go where My light is dim, where My voice is heard small, and My healing power is not known, even to the uttermost bounds of the earth. Their work will exceed yours, and in this I am well pleased."

Immediately, the focus of the Oral Roberts Evangelistic Association expanded. In 1961, a 160-acre farm was purchased in South Tulsa for $1,850 per acre.

The first announcement for the university was made by Roberts at a meeting of the Ministerial Alliance of Tulsa on December 5, 1961.

After receiving title to the land, architects were hired, educational consultants were brought on board, and major fundraising began. Thousands of Roberts's "partners" caught the vision and enough money was received that an official groundbreaking ceremony was held in February, 1962.

For the next three years, construction was non-stop, and by the fall of 1965, seven major buildings were completed and the doors were ready to open.

The initial freshman class included 303 students from across the nation and foreign countries. On September 7, 1965, a "Quest for the Whole Man" school-opening dinner was attended by over 600 students, faculty, and guests. The *Tulsa World* quoted Roberts as telling the audience, "Wholeness is...here. It's something you can get—it's something you can become. It's yours and it's waiting. It's not to come to you. You will have to lay hold of it and take it."

He added, "ORU is a daring new concept in higher education. It was planned to be from the beginning—one that would be able and willing to innovate change in all three basic aspects of your being—the intellectual, the physical, and the spiritual."

In a rather bold statement, Roberts told the freshmen they could emerge "as the world's most wanted college graduates."

During the next few years, the university reached major milestones and received national attention. The first graduates were awarded their diplomas in 1969. Just two years later ORU received accreditation from the Higher Learning Commission of the North Central Association of Colleges and Schools.

Enrollment grew from the hundreds to the thousands. The curriculum expanded too, with undergraduate programs in business, music, theology, communication arts, modern languages, behavioral sciences, graphics, education, biology, chemistry, computer science, mathematical science, engineering, physics, English, history, humanities, government, and nursing. In addition, the university also added a graduate seminary and fully accredited graduate programs in business and education.

More buildings emerged, including the 11,000-seat Mabee Center, home to sports, concerts, and other major events.

ORU also made headlines on the sports pages, competing at the highest division of the NCAA. Many of its athletes achieved outstanding professional careers after being drafted by the National Basketball Association and Major League Baseball.

THE CITY OF FAITH

Were there challenges? Plenty.

A pivotal moment in the history of the university was the announcement by Oral Roberts that he planned to build what he called the "City of Faith" on an 80-acre site across the street from ORU.

To many, it seemed a paradox that a man who built his ministry on faith-healing would create a medical center where trained physicians and surgeons would practice. But Roberts believed that every healing act is an instrument of God, and this facility would merge the healing streams of prayer and medicine.

The announcement took the medical establishment in Oklahoma by surprise and the hospitals in the region did their best to block the project. But in April 1978, the

Oklahoma Health Planning Commission approved the endeavor. As reported in the *Tulsa World,* within two hours after Oral Roberts was given the go-ahead, "heavy equipment roared into place on the South Tulsa site and began construction."

What emerged was a 60-story clinic and diagnostic center, a 30-story full-service hospital, and a 20-story research center. The clinic opened in 1981 with nine physicians and grew to 80 (all with faculty appointments to the Oral Roberts School of Medicine). Its first patients were accepted that November and the facility was certified for 294 beds (Oral envisioned it eventually growing to 777). At the same time, the research center was focusing on cancer, heart disease, arthritis, diabetes, and geriatrics.

Many looked into the future and saw the City of Faith as "the Mayo of the Southwest."

But it was not to be. Instead of drawing patients from across the country as expected, the majority of the beds remained empty. According to public records, the yearly losses were millions of dollars—and the gap wasn't being closed by donations from supporters of the Oral Roberts Evangelistic Association.

In early September, 1989, with a heavy heart, Roberts announced that the hospital and ORU Medical School were closing. According to documents filed with the federal Health

Care Financing Administration, from its opening until the end of fiscal year 1989, the City of Faith lost $59.7 million in operating costs.

On the academic side, ORU continues to have an outstanding pre-med program with its students accepted at more than 70 medical schools nationally, including Johns Hopkins University, Washington University, and Duke University. Over 300 ORU alumni are practicing physicians in the United States. Plus, its Anna Vaughn College of Nursing is recognized as one of the best in America.

In addition to the City of Faith becoming a severe financial drain on the university, during the same years, the School of Law also became a casualty. It opened in 1979, but became involved in an expensive court battle with the American Bar Association that took issue with ORU's Code of Honor pledge. It finally won accreditation, but the cost of operation was adding to the school's mounting debt. In 1986 the decision was made to close the school and give the 190,000 volume law library to Pat Roberton's CBN University (now Regent University). Five faculty and 23 law students also moved to Virginia.

By 1988, more than 10,000 students had graduated from ORU, and even with its severe financial problems, there was a dedicated faculty who believed in the original vision, and students continued to be drawn to a campus that offered a "whole person" education.

During the 1990s and into the 21st century, the university continued to face headwinds, yet survived.

Then came the crisis of 2007.

3

NO TIME TO WASTE

T he Green proposal was officially presented, and the decision to accept or reject now lay in the hands of the Board of Regents.

Dr. Cooley had to rush to the airport to catch his flight that Monday afternoon, January 14, 2008, but asked Mart Green to phone him with any news. The moment Cooley's plane touched the tarmac in Charlotte, he saw that Green had been trying to contact him. When they connected, Mart could hardly wait to say, "The Regents voted to accept our proposal—100 percent—and the entire board resigned. We're ready to move ahead."

"We have no time to waste," replied Cooley, "It's important that we put a new Board of Trustees together immediately."

The following day, the Regents created a temporary board to aid the coming transition, and Green announced that Ralph Fagin, Executive Vice President for Academic Affairs, would serve as interim president.

The process of creating a Board of Trustees included input from several entities—ORU alumni, the Greens, Cooley, and others. In the next few days, the proposed list was vetted and phone calls of invitation were made. Not one invitee turned the offer down, and the new board was asked to meet at ORU just a few days later, on January 28.

Mart Green was hesitant regarding being named Chairman of the Board, but was finally convinced that since his father and the Green family had taken such a step of faith in providing financial resources, it was fitting that he should lead the initial board.

In addition to Mart Green, the proposed list of new trustees included:

- Dr. Don H. Argue, former President of the National Association of Evangelicals
- Mary Banks, President W.O.W. Consulting Group
- Jay Betz, executive, Dollar Thrifty Automotive Group
- Fredrick A. Boswell, Jr., Executive Director of SIL, a faith-based linguistic organization
- Dr. Stanley Burgess, Professor Emeritus, Missouri State University
- Dr. Scott Cordray, D.O. surgeon
- Hal Donaldson, President, Convoy of Hope
- Rick Fenimore, ORU graduate, President, Trinity Chemical Industries

- Michael Hammer, businessman, philanthropist
- Rob Hoskins, President of Global Scripture Ministry, One Hope
- Scott Howard, ORU graduate, President of Commercial Roofers
- Lynette (Troyer) Lewis, ORU graduate, author and speaker
- Ron Luce, ORU graduate, founder of Teen Mania Ministries
- Dr. Charles McKinney, consultant, former Director of Educational Services, Florida Gulf Coast University
- Dr. Glenda Payas, ORU graduate, Tulsa dentist
- Dr. Russell Spittler, Provost Emeritus, Fuller Theological Seminary

Vice Chair of the Trustees would be William (Billy) Wilson, former Executive Director for the International Center for Spiritual Renewal and Chair of the worldwide Empowered21 Initiative.

Oral Roberts would serve as a lifetime member.

A few of the new trustees had been former business regents and alumni. Mart Green commented, "This gave us some 'institutional memory.'"

The Calling of a Steward

At the first official meeting of the new Board of Trustees,

each member was handed a large three-ring binder—their handbook for the task ahead. Among other items, it contained the Articles of Incorporation, bylaws, fiduciary responsibilities, charters for committees, financial information, policies and procedures, and much more.

Most important was a charge regarding "The Ministry of Trusteeship." It read:

Election to the Board of Trustees of Oral Roberts University is an invitation to a sacred trust; the roots of that trust are biblical. From those roots rise our mission as the university's Board and our ministry as individual Trustees. After God concluded His creative work and pronounced it "very good," He charged mankind with the responsibility of serving as "trustees" and "stewards" of all His creation.

The mission of the Board of Trustees is to be stewards; stewards of the physical resources, stewards of the intellectual climate, stewards of human relationships, and stewards of spiritual resources.

Within the mission of the Board the individual Trustee finds his or her ministry in response to the call of God. In this response to the divine call upon our lives, we commit to a common faith. We are also called to recognize and cultivate our individual gifts.

University Trustees find ministry in their roles when their calling to common faith and cultivation of individual gifts is focused upon a special task uniquely their own; to fulfill his or her calling and find meaning in ministry, every Trustee has work to do.

With the appointment of each new board member, they were reminded that trusteeship at ORU is an honor and a privilege:

- It is an honor because an invitation to serve is an affirmation that the university, as a collective body, is willing to entrust its future, in large part, to the judgment, work, and resources of the persons selected.
- It is a privilege because the opportunity to help ensure the future of a university is offered to very few outstanding men and women.

WOULD THE VISION CONTINUE?

One of the major sticking points in the transition from a Board of Regents to a Board of Trustees was Oral Roberts's insistence that his son be on the reconstituted board. Even though Richard had resigned as president, Oral wanted him to somehow be involved in the future of the university. At one informal meeting with the Greens at Oral's on-campus home, he made the statement, "God put my son in there, and no man is going to take him out."

This was a non-starter for the new leadership, and Oral finally realized that a fresh beginning, with new faces, was absolutely necessary.

At the January 28 meeting, the Board of Trustees was made official, and their first order of business was a vote to approve a new set of bylaws for the university.

The Greens also affirmed the remaining $62 million of their $70 million gift.

Throughout the transition, one question repeatedly surfaced. It was asked by former Regents, faculty, alumni, and donors: "Will the vision and purpose given to Oral Roberts for the university continue to be central in the days and years ahead?"

That question was addressed squarely in the new bylaws. Article II, section 2.1, Purposes:

The University is formed to establish, maintain, and conduct a university for the promotion and advancement of education and higher learning and to confer such degrees and grant such honors as are usually and customarily conferred in accredited institutions.

The University is founded upon and shall forever be dedicated to the promulgation and preservation of Biblical Christianity and academic excellence. The University is a Christian institution with the distinctive Charismatic dimension of the Holy Spirit. The expression of the gifts and fruit of the Holy Spirit is to be encouraged.

The University seeks to educate the whole person with balanced emphasis placed on the development of mind, spirit, and body, harmonizing knowledge, skills, and attitudes with faith in, and commitment to, Jesus Christ as Lord and Savior, believing Him to be the only perfect, whole person who has lived.

The University is committed to the historic Christian faith of the eternal Godhead: Father, Son, and Holy Spirit who, through the new birth and indwelling of us as believers by His Spirit, is Lord of our lives now and forever.

The University is committed to assist students in their quest for knowledge of their personal relationship to God, to mankind, and to the universe in which we live. Dedicated to the realization of truth as it is totally embodied in Christ and the achievement of one's potential life capacity, the University seeks to graduate an integrated person: a person spiritually alive, intellectually alert, physically disciplined in his work on earth, and living at all times in expectancy of the Second Coming of Christ.

To accomplish these purposes, the University seeks to synthesize, by means of interdisciplinary cross-pollination, the best traditions in liberal arts, professional, and graduate education with a Charismatic concern of the Holy Spirit himself to enable students to go into every man's world with God's healing power to help meet the totality of human need.

SEMINARY CONCERNS

This document was especially significant to ORU's seminary—The Oral Roberts University Graduate School of Theology and Missions. (Later the word "Missions" was changed to "Ministry.")

Dr. Thomson Mathew, who had been dean of the school since 2000, admitted that when the new leadership arrived, the seminary naturally had concerns about the university's spiritual direction. "In the beginning we didn't know what we were signing up for." But when he and the seminary faculty met the academicians who had such rich backgrounds in theological education on the Board of Trustees, he realized the benefits of their support. He said, "They enhance our work."

Mathew noted, "The School's curriculum remains unapologetically Charismatic in conviction and commitment —and balanced. We teach the whole counsel of God— everything God wants us to know to live the kingdom life-style."

Joy Ames, a 2008 M.Div. graduate, commented, "If someone approached me and asked about ORU's spiritual direction, I would assure them that the Holy Spirit is still alive and active on the campus. I am proud to be a graduate of ORU's School of Missions. If asked if I would do it again, there is no question; the answer is 'Yes.'"

SEPARATE ENTITIES?

A matter that needed urgent attention centered around the fact that the Oral Roberts Evangelistic Association and ORU were virtually inseparable—linked together like conjoined twins. From the very beginning, OREA donors supported the ministry and the university financially as if they were one entity. Since any actions on the part of the Association impacted the university, the new trustees felt a firewall needed to be built between the two.

There was one early document that stated OREA could be

physically housed on the university campus forever.

The iconic 200-foot glass-and-steel Prayer Tower in the center of the campus opened in 1967. It was where volunteers received thousands of phone calls worldwide from men and women requesting prayer.

Richard Roberts had a valid argument. There would be substantial costs involved in relocating OREA off campus.

The trustees and Roberts reached an agreement that gave OREA the funds to move off campus and keep the prayer line phone number. At the same time, the names of donors who had designated their gifts specifically to ORU would remain with the university so there would be a base for future financial support.

The trustees were also committed to honor donors to the ministry who had given their time and treasure to the spiritual training of young people.

As you can imagine, the dynamic changes that were taking place at ORU shifted the rumor mill among students and alumni into overdrive. There were some who said, "With all the negative headlines the school has received, I heard that the trustees are considering changing the name of Oral Roberts University to something else."

Nothing could be further from the truth. In fact, the restated "Certificate of Incorporation" filed with the Oklahoma Secretary of State, Article X, 10.2 specifies that the name of the university "shall not be altered or amended except upon approval by a vote of 100% of the whole Board of Trustees at each of three consecutive annual meetings of the Board."

That issue was settled.

A NECESSARY CATALYST

Ralph Fagin was a natural choice to be the interim president. He had spent 36 years at ORU, including being a student, graduate, sociology professor, Provost, and had announced his retirement. Observed Mart Green, "We were looking for an insider who was respected by the faculty but who did not wish to be considered for the permanent presidency post."

Fagin became a necessary catalyst between the old and the new.

About a week after his appointment, the faculty and their families were invited to a semi-formal dinner. Ralph Fagin and the Greens shared their hearts regarding the future of the university. In a video, Chancellor Oral Roberts expressed his peace to the faculty about the direction ORU was headed. Hearing those words was extremely powerful to those who had entrusted their professional lives to the university.

LISTENING, LEARNING, LAUNCHING

Starting that January, Mart Green began spending two or three days every week on campus, talking with students, listening to faculty, and chatting with staff members.

In early spring, signs were posted at various locations, letting everyone know about specific renovations that would be taking place before school reopened in August. New furniture, lifts for those with physical challenges, refinished porches, new elevators, and—students really liked this one—a micro-fridge in every dorm room.

Off campus, Mart Green held a series of meetings with alumni and began making phone calls to talk with former graduates. "Almost to a person," he said, "they started by bragging about the school as they knew it...then they expressed their dismay at some of the negatives that had been reported in the press."

One concern was voiced again and again. It was the fact that for several years there had been major fundraising efforts to build the proposed Armand Hammer Alumni-Student Center. But this never materialized because of the financial drain caused by the school's escalating debt service.

Many felt this was a major contributing factor of why alumni giving had been on a downward spiral.

Immediately, the Greens made the necessary moves to

give the project priority. What would be the impact of a promise fulfilled? How would students and alumni respond when they would eventually see bulldozers leveling the ground for the foundation of the first major building on campus in 30 years?

The answer would come later.

WHY ORU?

The commencement speaker for the 2008 graduating class was Kelly Wright, the Fox News anchor. He wasn't selected for his honors as a reporter, rather because he was personally becoming a graduate of ORU that day.

Wright had been a student 30 years earlier, but left to serve in the U.S. Army before his broadcasting career. He is also an ordained minister and Gospel recording artist. However, his dream to finish his degree didn't die, and he earned the necessary credits to not only be handed his diploma, but also deliver the major address that day. He spoke of the influence ORU had on his life.

The response to Wright's presentation at the packed Mabee Center was given by Jamie Weathers, a government major who graduated Summa Cum Laude. Those present will never forget her powerful address. It, once and for all, answered the question, "Why ORU?"

Here are Jamie's remarks—which should be read by any student thinking about where to receive a college education:

Despite what may be true at other universities, there are three parts of a man—spirit, mind, and body. Together they make up the whole man. And in a world that wants to separate the three parts of man, either by ignoring one or worshiping another, we here at ORU understand the necessity of becoming this whole man. And this is why I believe that you, the graduating class of 2008, have received the best education in the world.

Now you may be thinking, "Wait a minute. Have you ever heard of Harvard, Yale, Cambridge, or Oxford?" Yes, I have—and I've even attended one briefly. But I say to you that the education you have received at Oral Roberts University is far superior to any of those. This is because your education has been infused with the Word of God, from which comes biblical morality and absolute truth.

Socrates, one of the greatest philosophers and educators of antiquity believed in the existence of absolute truth. It is also said that he thought morality and virtue were some of the greatest accomplishments of man, because without morality based on absolute truth one would be unable to reason, and we can see this in the postmodern society that we live in today, where there is no right and there is no wrong.

I ask, how in the absence of absolutes can we expect people to make the logical decisions in a society that says faith cannot be married with reason and the Bible cannot be linked with logic?

I'm sure most of you here today have been asked on one or more occasions, why go to a Christian university? Why go to ORU? Because at ORU we believe that the pursuit of knowledge is ultimately acquainted with the pursuit of God, and it is by the discipline of our spirit, mind, and body that we are able to fulfill the call that is on our lives. I truly believe that it is only by knowing absolute truth and understanding biblical morality that we are able to reason in this world.

Paul spoke of a world ever learning, and searching for knowledge, yet never able to come to the knowledge of truth. In that world, my friends, you have the answers.

You have been given a whole education that does not shy away from asking the deeper questions that challenge our faith—a whole education that does not seek to omit theory, but rather requires the discipline to discern whether these theories properly reflect the Word of God. A whole education that matures your spirit, challenges your mind, and even strengthens your body.

My friends, it is this whole education that has equipped you to be the leaders and problem-solvers, the ministers to the nations and to the rest of the world. What this world needs is whole men and whole women. I tell you:

It takes a whole man to just meet the needs of others in his home and community and to be used by God to meet those needs.

It takes a whole woman to go to Wall Street and come up with creative and ethical business solutions for a struggling economy.

It takes a whole man to teach in the classrooms of America filled with children from broken homes who are in desperate need of love.

It takes a whole woman to leave the comforts of the Western world and go to a foreign land with an unknown language and bring the Word of God.

It takes a whole man to come up with the technological advances that will relieve the nations of extreme poverty and mass starvation.

It will take a whole woman to march up the steps of Capitol Hill with her head held high, ready to bring integrity and justice to the political realm.

It will take a whole man to be inspired by the Holy Spirit to make masterpiece works of literature, art, and music that reflect the beauty and existence of God.

It will take a whole woman to care for patients, cure disease, to lay hands on the sick and raise the dead.

(Then glancing at Mart Green) It took a whole man to obey God and give over 70 million dollars!

It will take a whole woman who is unsure of her future to wait on the voice of the Lord to tell her what to do tomorrow.

It will take a whole man to hear His voice, to go where the light is dim and His voice is heard small, and His healing power is not known even to the uttermost bounds of the earth.

And, my friends, it will take all of you—whole men and whole women—to stand up right now and give all the glory to God.

DRAMATIC CHANGES

The campus crisis of 2007 sent shock waves through the admissions office. That fall, with headlines predicting gloom and doom for ORU, many students had already made up their minds to transfer, and some withdrew their applications. Even with the announcement that there had been a major financial rescue and a new board was in place, the turn-around was not instantaneous. The numbers told the story. The Fall 2007 enrollment was 3,166, but it dropped to 3,067 the next year.

The students who *did* return saw dramatic changes on campus. That summer ORU had its $10.4 million facelift —new flowers and shrubs, fresh carpets in many classrooms, reupholstered furniture, top-to-bottom remodeling of two major dorms, and so much more. Returning junior Alyssa Bailey commented, "It means a beginning. It encourages you to keep going. It gives me new life and new hope."

Even more surprised were alums who were bringing the next generation to campus. Nan (Stoskoph-87) Gammill and her husband Dana (1983-87) brought their son, Michael, a freshman. A visit by the parents two years earlier had left them saddened by the physical condition of the campus. But now it was different. Nan exclaimed, "You can imagine my amazement upon my arrival on August 8, 2008. I was very impressed and so set at ease by all that I saw happening." She continued, "All the renovations blew me away. I couldn't believe so much had been accomplished in so short a period of time."

In addition to the physical changes, the alum stated, "I was incredibly blessed to see that Oral's vision is not only being preserved, but promoted to a whole new level." She added, "I was deeply encouraged and convinced that we had nothing to fear. ORU is alive and well and ready for all whom God has called there, including our son."

4

SHARED GOVERNANCE

T he campus was buzzing with optimism and excitement when the Board of Trustees met on campus for their second meeting, May, 2008—coinciding with graduation.

In addition to formalizing the new board, a major order of business was to approve a mission statement for the university, from which all other decisions and actions would flow. The statement now reads:

> *To build Holy Spirit-empowered leaders*
> *through whole person education to impact*
> *the world with God's healing.*

If the trustees thought their role was honorary and their duties were simply to attend scheduled meetings, they were in for a surprise. Chairman Mart Green let them know that this would be a "working" board, with each member having specific assignments.

They were organized into five teams:

1. Academic Affairs
2. Student Affairs
3. Leadership
4. Finance
5. Advancement

There were three or four trustees on each team...and those numbers expanded as the board grew.

From that point forward, this impacted the agenda. There was a plenary session where the university president gave a report and opening statement. Then the teams would meet to work on their individual agendas, and would bring in liaisons from the administration. For example, the Academic Affairs Committee invited the provost, and the Finance Committee brought in the CFO.

Their immediate task was to create resolutions and recommendations to the entire board. These became vibrant sessions and brought efficiency to the process.

A NEW CONCEPT

A few weeks earlier, Mart Green addressed the alumni at their February Homecoming. During his forward-looking remarks, he stated that "shared governance" was a prerequi-site for his family's generous financial gift.

This was a new concept on campus, and it took considerable time for the faculty, alumni, administration, and the trustees to understand what it truly encompassed.

Since its founding, ORU had been guided by autocratic leadership that reflected the vision of its founder. In truth, the school would not have made such rapid strides any other way. But this was a new day—and going forward there would be *many* stakeholders involved in decision-making.

Mart Green asked Dr. Cooley to share the concept in detail at several early trustee meetings. Cooley explained, "The goal of shared governance is to safeguard the educational mission of ORU while maintaining its economic vitality."

The guiding principles require:

- Mutual respect of the university's governance groups while recognizing the different levels of authority.
- Acknowledging that many may speak to an issue while reserving the right of some to make a decision which is inherent in their area of responsibility.
- Developing and sustaining the school's policies, decision-making structures, and plans that balance the interest and goals of the various individuals and groups within ORU and in its external constituency.

- Maintaining formal and informal information systems for transparent feedback, communication, and interaction within the university.
- Upholding and supporting the president's role as gatekeeper and facilitator of the governance process.

While that was the theory, what the trustees and other stakeholders wanted to know was, "How does this work in practice?"

They learned that, in the new ORU, the faculty would have functional authority for the entire educational program—and be in charge of the academics of the school. So the faculty now had *functional* authority.

The president, who had delegated authority, would build the administrative team, and they too would function under *delegated* authority—with the board having *final* authority. This meant that any recommendation for any major university-wide policy had to rise up through the system to the board—and the trustees would have to sign off on the matter.

In this newly-adopted shared governance model, reciprocity between the president and the Board of Trustees is mutual. The president becomes the gatekeeper of this shared governance process and the key facilitator. The faculty, with its functional authority, gives input into the educational process. Thus, the shared authority process flows from the faculty, to the president, to the board, back to the president, then to the faculty.

PRIORITIES

The board had a set of priorities to fulfill:

- First, they were committed to safeguard the school's mission in their decisions.
- Second, they were responsible for selecting and caring for the president.
- Third, they were accountable for the financial condition of ORU.
- Fourth, they were responsible for the physical property and the onward strategic planning of the university.

The trustees also learned that shared governance was a self-corrective process. For example, if the faculty made a recommendation that the board could not accept, the trustees would return the recommendation to the faculty, with reasons for their concern. This was a negotiated process, not "my way or the highway."

This also applied to the board. If the trustees made certain decisions that upset the faculty, there would be horizontal conversations taking place. Says Cooley, "The system we set in place included that all actions of each entity would be communicated to the other parties, so there was never a question of who should be notified." Shared governance is an information system.

Mart Green observed, "With the stakeholder renewal, there has been a sense of ownership on the part of everybody. The focus was no longer on a founder or a personality, but there was an agreed-upon set of educational values that bonded the community together—and that is what drives ORU."

The new trustees were enthusiastic about the role of shared governance in the direction of the school. Dr. Russell Spittler, with a Ph.D. from Harvard and years of experience in leading Christian colleges and seminaries, said, "When you build a large building you have to go down before you can go up"—and he was ready to help rebuild ORU. He was convinced that, for the university to establish a reputation for superior academic quality, it needed right governance to accompany able administration, qualified faculty, and eager students. "What has happened is an astonishing development," Spittler added.

The response from the faculty was expressed by Dr. Kenneth Weed, Dean of the College of Science and Engineering: "It's fantastic because the trustees, the Office of the President, and the University Planning Council are all in the same room talking," he said. "Faculty are free to come up with creative ideas. We can't do them all, but that's okay. Amongst all these new ideas are going to be some that are revolutionary, breaking through and helping to frame the future of ORU."

BALANCING THE BUDGET

Those who thought that the $70 million gift from the Green family would be a never-ending funnel of funds that would keep the university financially solvent in the future were mistaken. In April, 2008, the university announced that up to 100 of the approximately 700 employees would be laid off within the next few months. "We can't spend more than we bring in," explained Mart Green, chairman of the board. He added, "While we regret that the reduction in force is necessary, it is imperative that the ORU Board of Trustees and management be prudent and good stewards of the university's resources."

When the reductions occurred, it affected staff rather than faculty. Those impacted were given a 60-day notification period and placement support.

THE SEARCH

While Ralph Fagin was doing a remarkable job as Interim

President, the trustees knew that a permanent leader needed to be in place as soon as possible. The Presidential Search Committee spent literally hundreds of hours vetting 130 names that had been submitted by alumni, faculty, church leaders, and academicians.

The name that rose to the surface was Dr. Mark Rutland, then President of Southeastern University, an Assemblies of God institution in Lakeland, Florida.

Rutland and Oral Roberts shared one thing in common: they had both been Methodists. While Rutland completed his studies at Emory University, he pastored Little River United Methodist Church in Woodstock, Georgia, and later was the minster of Oak Grove United Methodist in Atlanta.

Roberts had been raised in the Pentecostal Holiness denomination, but joined the Methodist church in Tulsa in 1968.

Rutland had a personal Pentecostal experience in 1975 that eventually led him to pastor Calvary Assembly of God church in Orlando, Florida—which doubled in size under his leadership. Then, in 1999, he was asked to become president of Southeastern University, a school that was struggling financially and suffering from declining enrollment. During his ten-year tenure, the school's enrollment increased from 1,000 to more than 3,000, and saw more than $50 million invested in new construction and renovation projects on campus.

The announcement that Rutland had accepted ORU's invitation was made at the January, 2009 trustee meeting ...and that he would begin his service as president in July.

Rutland said that when Board Chair Mart Green first approached him to consider the ORU presidency, he wasn't interested. Before long, however, "I came to an awareness of His purpose" and made the decision to come to ORU.

"In leadership," he explained, "where lightning strikes is where need and opportunity intersect. You can have plenty of need, but if there is no opportunity to change it, the need just swats your boat. But when need and opportunity cross, right in that intersection, that is where excitement and energy happen. And there was plenty of need and no shortage of opportunity, and that intersection is what attracted me."

EMBRACING THE TRANSITION

Oral Roberts, over the objections of his medical doctors in California, made a trip to Tulsa that February to speak to the alumni at Homecoming. At 91 years old, he assured those present that the university he founded was in good hands with the family of Mart Green: "It was as if we'd known each other all our lives," Roberts said. "And they picked it up and never missed a beat."

61

Mart stated that from the early days of the transition, Roberts was supportive. "I was thrilled by that, because he'd been at this for a long, long time, and I just came in at the very end. And to be grafted in so quickly—he embraced me as well as my family. That's what gave me the strength to make it." He added, "Without his support I'm sure I would have been faint of heart."

Oral was also delighted about the prospect of Mark Rutland becoming president. "He will have a great opportunity to excel and take this school to a new level," he commented.

As a *Tulsa World* reporter wrote, "He embraced the transition to shared governance and praised ORU's faculty and students for wanting to help decide how the university is run."

Mart Green told those gathered, "This is a healing university, and the deepest wound is where the flower grows. In Corinthians, it tells us God heals and then He brings someone alongside us so that He can heal them. That's part of what we can do here at ORU. Some have scars that are not healed yet. It's going to take time. Some of you are excited about ORU, but be patient. The train's left the station. Some are going to get on now, some are going to board later—but they're going to get on this train. We need your help. We're all in this together."

A QUIET PLACE

The Homecoming was significant for another reason. The Prayer Tower, which had been closed when the Abundant Life prayer group and OREA had moved off campus a year earlier, was refurbished and rededicated.

At the ceremony, Roberts observed, "If I could name the one thing that ORU is best noted for: the presence of God." He remarked that he built the Prayer Tower in the middle of the campus "so the presence of God could not be escaped."

He also told the gathering, "I would visit the tower whenever I faced a difficult situation, and once spent three straight days and nights here."

While the ringing phones were now silent and the fluorescent lights in the tower's prayer room were long gone, the renovated room was designed as a quiet haven where students and staff could get away from the bustle of campus life to pray.

Many observers credit Roberts with bringing the Charismatic movement into the mainstream of religion in the United States and abroad. He was honored and respected as a man of integrity and invited to speak at major interdenominational events worldwide. During this visit, however, the founder of ORU said, "Creating the university was the crowning achievement of my life."

Ten months later, in Southern California, Oral Roberts died of complications from pneumonia on December 15, 2009.

5

A VISION RENEWED

In February 2008, the trustees approved an alumni fundraising campaign named "Renewing the Vision." The objective was to raise $25 million before May, 2009. The funds would be used for student recruitment and retention, scholarships and other financial aid, plus campus renovations, refurbishments, and upgrades.

The campaign included a "bonus." The trustees announced they would match every dollar up to $25 million—and designate those funds toward retiring the university's debt.

During that year, the alumni caught the excitement of the new ORU and first-time alumni donors soared from 179 to 679. It was the highest alumni giving since 1998.

There was increasing confidence that the university was headed in the right direction. One of the early goals of the Board of Trustees was to gain membership in the Evangelical Council for Financial Accountability (ECFA). The group admits only non-profits that comply with strict standards for bookkeeping, fundraising, and leadership. ORU received its seal of approval in March, 2009.

At the end of the highly successful 14-month campaign, the trustees announced that not only had the university eliminated its long term debt, but had received financial gifts from approximately 15,000 donors.

Natalie Bounds-Adams, Director of Alumni Relations at the time, voiced, "It isn't about the money as much as it's about relationship-building with alums."

The trustees became a working board, the faculty was grateful for shared governance, alumni giving was on the rise, and campus renovation projects were underway. But how would all this impact the real barometer of success: enrollment?

THE "QUEST"

The board was well aware that enrollment was a matter that needed serious attention—and they took immediate action. With a matching grant offered by the Green family, what is now called the "Quest Whole Person Scholarship" was created and announced in 2008.

Nominations for the scholarship were opened to freshmen and transfer students planning to attend ORU in the fall of 2009. Students could be nominated by school, church, and community leaders, or an ORU alumnus, faculty, or staff member. The qualifications were designed to award students who exemplify the "whole person" lifestyle—demonstrating proficiencies and capacities in being spiritually alive, intellectually alert, physically disciplined, socially adept, and professionally competent.

The word "Quest" has a special meaning at ORU. It was the title of Oral Roberts's inaugural chapel message, "Quest for the Whole Man" when the school's doors opened in 1965, and this concept is foundational to understanding ORU's core values. Roberts preached, "The model is Jesus Christ, the only whole person who *'grew in wisdom and stature, and in favor with God and man'"* (Luke 3:52). And he often referred to 1 Thessalonians 5:23: *"[May the] God of peace sanctify you wholly; and I pray God your whole spirit and soul and body be preserved blameless unto the coming of our Lord Jesus Christ."*

From these scriptures, Roberts derived the goals of developing the mind through education, the body through physical exercise, and the spirit through spiritual disciplines under the guidance of the Holy Spirit.

The program opened the door to a significant recruiting opportunity and drew hundreds of prospective students to the campus.

As a result of the 2009 competition, 31 students were awarded full-tuition scholarships (worth $18,476 each at the time) and over 450 students were granted partial scholarships.

The program is now a permanent part of the university's future.

BUILDING BRIDGES

Mark Rutland, who had been named as ORU's third president, arrived on campus July 1, 2009. On his first day in office he hit the ground running, meeting with department heads and staff, ready to begin implementing initiatives that had been discussed during the past few months. Said Rutland, "It's not my style to sit and maintain something. I want to be part of something that is moving, going, and growing, where there is excitement and energy. I feel that here, and I feel that it will gain."

Rutland also spoke of breaking down barriers between the university and the surrounding community. "I want to open up and lighten up...we're going to make things more user-friendly and more accessible," he said.

In these still-early days of the turnaround, there were many public relations questions that needed to be addressed, including: *What is the ORU image? How does the public perceive the university?*

After much discussion, the best answer was that the image

and visibility would depend on ORU itself. The product worth marketing was whole person education and mission fulfillment, not buildings, faculty, or activities.

From the day he took the reins, Rutland was tireless in reaching out to alumni, pastors, and potential students across the nation with the story of the new ORU.

In addition, he began rebuilding bridges that had been damaged between the campus and the community. With the major changes taking place at ORU, the city fathers were more than willing to extend their hands. Rutland was invited to address the Chamber of Commerce, civic clubs, trade groups, educational organizations, and more.

This was good news to Douglas Fears, a trustee who was added to the board in January, 2009. Fears was executive vice president and CFO of Helmerich & Payne, a NYSE-listed, Tulsa-based contract drilling company.

As the father and father-in-law of two ORU graduates, he was more than familiar with the university. His financial background made him a natural choice to chair the audit committee. Fears noted that the group's mandate is "to ensure there is integrity in the financial systems and the finanancial reports." He added, "Anybody that cares about the university should feel total confidence that the financial records and the internal controls are done professionally, accurately, with honesty and integrity and transparency."

Fears sees ORU as an asset to Tulsa. He said, "You would be surprised and encouraged if you knew how many people came up to me and said the same thing over and over, and that was, 'I'm so excited about what is going on at ORU'...There's great enthusiasm within Tulsa...for ORU's success."

CONQUERING THE DRAGONS

With Rutland at the helm, there was a second summer of campus upgrades, thanks to another $10 million gift from the Green family. Board Chair Mart Green had said that deferred maintenance was one of the four "dragons" that ORU must defeat in order to achieve "mission with economic sustainability." The other three dragons were debt, declining enrollment, and deficit.

This time the renovations included, among other projects, upgrades for the chemistry labs, baseball stadium, Aerobics Center, Christ's Chapel, Mabee Center, and cafeteria. A major addition to the campus was the privately funded 35,000-square-foot indoor practice facility attached to the Golden Eagle Sports Complex. The $1.2 million project caters to baseball, track, and soccer teams, and features an artificial surface infield, including a pitcher's mound and bases, three batting cages, and can house indoor track and field training and events with its pole vault area, plus a variety of jump pits. It had plenty of "wow" factors for recruiting and developing quality student athletes.

When the school opened in Fall 2009, enrollment had increased to 3,140, representing 40 states and 56 countries. Most importantly, new student enrollment had risen from 766 in 2008 to 902—more than a 17% jump.

On a humorous note, at the September 15 luncheon of the Alumni Connection, Dr. Rutland spoke of receiving a "Certificate of Death" from the Enrollment Management team. It read, "This is to certify the death of The Dragon of Declining Enrollment as witnessed this day, August 26, 2009, on the campus of Oral Roberts University. The dragon died of supernatural causes."

THE ULTIMATE LEADER

A month into the new academic year, more than 4,000 were present at the Mabee Center for President Rutland's inauguration. It was a day filled with pomp and circumstance, and something more. Who could have imagined that 44 years after ORU was founded, Oral Roberts would be taking part in this event? Now quite frail, his entrance and exit were marked with heartfelt, loving shouts from the crowd, and standing ovations.

Rutland was welcomed by Marilyn Hickey, who chaired

the former Board of Regents for 19 years, and representatives from the Student Association, Faculty Senate, and Alumni Association. Salutations also came from Paul Corts, president of the Council of Christian Colleges and Universities, and Tulsa Mayor Kathy Taylor.

In his remarks, Dr. Rutland said, "I am deeply aware that I come as a Johnny-come-lately to a great university already in progress, a tank that is moving across the prairie. I may jump on and ride for a season. I probably will not change the tank much nor help it or hinder it. It was here before I got on and it will be rolling when I get off."

Regarding his role, Rutland remarked, "We are united under a leader that transcends us all. The ultimate leader of ORU is still Jesus Christ. It humbles us to understand that it is His pillar of fire, His cloud, His sword, His leadership, His calling, His university. We follow Him."

The moment those present will not forget is when Chancellor Oral Roberts laid his hands on a kneeling Mark Rutland and gave this prophetic prayer: "I see you leading this campus in the glory of God. I see you relating to all the faculty, the board, the students, ministering to them by the power of God and the Holy Word of God. I see you anointed by the Holy Ghost, set apart for this special ministry."

When Roberts returned to his home in California, he shared his feelings in a personal letter to Mart Green, one that the Green family will always cherish. It included: "What I saw and felt in my spirit is almost overwhelming. I had known that when the Robertses stepped aside that the Lord would continue to bless ORU and its great future." He continued, "I am at great peace now with you being board chair and the skillful way you are directing everything, including bringing us a new President. The real job that you have done is reflected throughout the campus. I thank God for you and everything you have done in my lifetime and will do in the future."

THE HOMEGOING

Three months later, on December 21, 2009, in that same Mabee Center, there would be another historical event. It was the memorial service for Oral Roberts, who had passed away a few days earlier. The story of his death was on the front page of more than 800 newspapers. Thousands were in attendance and the service was broadcast live worldwide on a variety of Christian television networks and internet sites.

In charge of the event was Richard Roberts. This was the first time he had been back on campus since his resignation two years earlier.

Oral's daughter, Roberta (Potts), shared how when she and her brother Richard went to the hospital just before their father died, "he was singing 'Something Good is Going to

Happen to You' at the top of his lungs, though he could barely move. Then he would stop for a while and add, 'I'm going home. I am going home. Hallelujah!'"

There were written tributes from Jimmy Carter, George H. W. Bush, and other notables from the worlds of entertainment, politics, and sports. Billy Graham wrote to Richard, "I will always treasure the last conversation I had with your father. I'm sure he heard the words 'Well done, good and faithful servant.'"

A year after the founder's passing Mark Rutland, in an interview with Bill Sherman, religion writer of the *Tulsa World,* said, "If one had to identify the enduring legacy of Oral Roberts as a man, that is certainly Oral Roberts University...and it's not just the bricks and mortar, it is the deep-tissue DNA of this university."

Rutland added, "Oral Roberts didn't just build a university, he built an idea, and that idea was whole-person education: mind, spirit, and body. Not leaving any of them out, and not letting any of them override the others. He was way ahead of his time."

A NAME OF REMEMBRANCE

In April 2010, the Avenue of Flags surrounding the iconic

Praying Hands at the entrance to the campus was renamed Billy Joe Daugherty Circle.

This was appropriate since he was held in such high regard as a graduate, a pastor, and the interim president at a critical time in the university's history. He was also founder of Victory Christian Center, a large sanctuary built across Lewis Avenue from ORU, with attendance at its Sunday services averaging over 9,000.

Sadly, he was diagnosed with non-Hodgkin's lymphoma and died at age 57 in November 2009.

At the dedication, his wife, Sharon, shared, "When his office across the street was first built, he wanted to face this Avenue of Flags so that he could see it every day and pray for ORU."

EXTRA HELP

Each summer, major renovation projects were underway, and 2010 was no different. This time, the major focus was on "eye appeal," making sure the campus grounds were in pristine condition. A long-term tree-planting plan was implemented and dorms were brought up to code ahead of new city fire regulations.

The most impressive physical improvement didn't cost ORU a dime. Fred Creek, a small stream that runs through the campus, had been an eyesore, but because of a Tulsa voter-approved General Obligation bond, $15 million was designated for rehab, including new landscaping, road work, plus a pedestrian bridge that connects the Mabee Center parking lot to the main campus.

In the midst of the enhancements taking place on campus, President Rutland made it clear that "the core values of our culture are the nonnegotiables, but the knick-knacks, the 'hows' and methods, our ways of doing things, are changing. We are striving to create an atmosphere of ingenuity, creativity, and experimentation. We are prepared to try new things, fail at some, improve others, and tinker with dials. Nomenclature is not sacred. Neither are style or titles. What is sacred is our commitment to Christ, our faithfulness to ORU's founding values, and our indomitable joy."

A Monumental Step

During Rutland's tenure, at a Homecoming chapel service in February 2011, he made the long-awaited announcement that the construction of the Armand Hammer Alumni-Student Center had been approved by the Board of Trustees. "For almost a decade, the ORU community has dreamt of this new student center. I am thrilled that dream is in hand," said Rutland. "This new facility is a monumental step in the continued revival of the university. This is a reminder of our legacy instilled by Chancellor Oral Roberts to 'expect a miracle.'"

The center received seed gifts of $8 million from the Armand Hammer Foundation and the Cardone Family Foundation, plus additional gifts from alumni to ensure completion of the $12 million project.

Groundbreaking took place at Homecoming 2012 and the impressive 28,000-square-foot building opened one year later—debt free. It is named to honor the original key gift to ORU from the Armand Hammer Foundation. Hammer was an oil tycoon and philanthropist associated with Occidental Petroleum.

Some have asked, "What was Armand Hammer's connection to ORU?"

It began when Hammer's grandson, Michael, became a Christian as an adult. While working at Occidental's Oklahoma offices, he met his future wife, Dru Ann Mobley, and they were married at the First Methodist Church in Tulsa.

At the dedication of the new alumni-student facility, Michael told how he was attending a conference in 2001 and learned of the need for a lead gift to launch a student center for the campus. "I felt God put that on my heart...and I said I would do it," recalled Hammer, chairman and CEO of the Armand Hammer Foundation.

Michael told the students how his life changed dramatically after he accepted Christ, and that his grandfather noticed the transformation. "He invited me to come and see him, and during our conversation my grandfather admitted to me, 'I need that peace.'"

During their visit, the famous 91-year-old began to weep, and asked Christ to be his Savior. He passed away the following year.

A portrait of the elder Hammer is displayed in the entryway of the building that bears his name.

The two-level state-of-the-art facility includes:

- Two dining options: Jazzman's Café and Moe's Southwestern Grill.
- Recreation: table tennis, billiards, air hockey, foosball, shuffleboard, electronic game consoles, and vintage arcade machines.
- A video wall 12 feet high by 21 feet wide. The largest television screen in Oklahoma at the time. The TV can display one single image for movie nights and sporting events, or can be broken up to project four separate screens to display the news, sports, movies, and social entertainment.
- Living room with fireplace—for general social and leisure activities.

- Quiet spaces for studying.
- Live performance areas.
- Workroom for group projects.
- Conference rooms and banquet space.
- A patio for outdoor dining and a fire pit.
- Outdoor games including disc golf, croquet, and lawn darts.

The second floor includes an Alumni Lounge, Development and Alumni offices, and conference rooms.

You can hear alums visiting the campus wistfully saying, "I wish this was here when I was a student!"

AN "ALL-STEINWAY" SCHOOL

In department after department, from business, communications, athletics, and science, there was growing optimism about the future—and the enthusiasm was accompanied by words such as "quality" and "excellence."

ORU's music department garnered headlines in March 2011 when it achieved the distinction of becoming an "All-Steinway School"—one of only a handful of Christian universities in the world to achieve this prestigious mark of distinction.

Steinway has the reputation of building the world's finest

pianos—and 37 new Steinways were purchased by a number of generous donors. One $60,000 gift allowed the school to purchase a 9-foot concert grand piano.

Concerning the designation, the dean of the ORU College of Arts and Cultural Studies commented, "Being an All-Steinway School will allow our students to work with the best pianos and will help attract future world-class musicians to the campus."

STEPPING DOWN

When Mark Rutland agreed to become president of ORU, he made it clear to the trustees that he did not consider the appointment his life's work, rather that he would commit several years to leading the university during this critical time of transition. So it did not come as a major surprise when, in the fall of 2011, Rutland announced his decision to step down from the school's leadership at the end of the 2012-2013 academic year.

At the graduation ceremony, May 4, 2013, he made his exit with the group of students he started with four years earlier. "It's like we're graduating at the same time," Rutland told them. "That's kind of rewarding."

During those four momentous years, the enrollment numbers were on a steady incline: 3,140, 3,212, 3,259, and 3,335.

ORU PRESIDENTS

Granville Oral Roberts
1965-1993

Richard Roberts
1993-2007

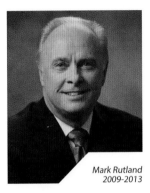

Mark Rutland
2009-2013

William M. Wilson
2013-Present

In 1962, the trustees of Oral Roberts Ministries broke ground on Oral Roberts University in South Tulsa.

Evelyn Roberts was a driving force behind the man, Oral Roberts.

A prayer of dedication over the 263 acres that would become ORU.

To lay the foundations for the first seven buildings, ORU had to dig deep.

Billy Graham delivered the address when ORU was dedicated in 1967.

ORU awarded its first diplomas in 1968.

Chapel has been an integral part of the ORU experience from the beginning.

ORU always strives to stay on the forefront of technology, and today's chapel services are no exception.

Students have fun while staying physically disciplined.

Students now come to ORU from all 50 states and over 100 nations.

ORU athletics teams compete at the Division I level.

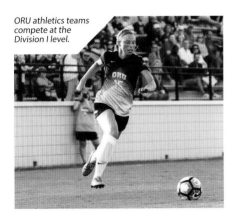

The iconic Praying Hands greet everyone who comes to ORU.

The ORU campus as it exists today.

The power of prayer was evident at Dr. William M. Wilson's inauguration.

J.L. Johnson Stadium, the home of ORU baseball since 1978, is a great place to catch a game.

Hobby Lobby founder David Green encourages graduates to put their "stakes in the ground" at ORU commencement.

ORU's annual RenewU revival is a cornerstone of the students' spiritual development.

Commencement always draws a large crowd to the 11,000-seat Mabee Center.

Students take full advantage of recreational activities in the Armand Hammer Alumni-Student Center (below).

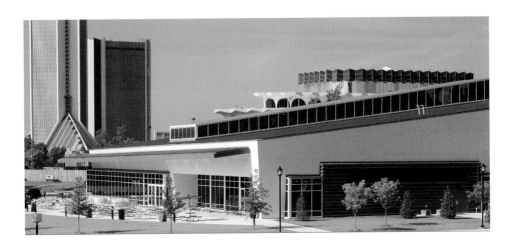

Mart Green congratulates Jamie Weathers upon graduation.

The athletics program teaches the joys of hard work and sportsmanship.

Dr. and Mrs. Wilson enjoy interacting with the ORU student body.

The 50th freshman class, joined by President and Mrs. Wilson, marked their arrival at ORU by forming a giant "50" on the lawn.

The Theater Department remains a strength in the ORU curriculum.

Prayer remains central at ORU, as evidenced by the student-led Prayer Movement, hosted in the Prayer Tower.

The Global Learning Center (below) officially opened in January, 2017.

Professors utilize AVR technology in the Global Learning Center.

Studies indicate that an AVR environment enhances a student's learning capacity up to 400%.

ORU has a strong foundation in finely tuned musical performance that continues to this day.

Part of the five-year adaptive plan is to increase ORU students' contributions to cutting-edge research.

The ONEOK Sports Complex for track and tennis is ORU's newest addition.

Prior to leading ORU, Rutland had authored 14 books, and planned to continue his writing. In addition, he would spend time developing his international missions work, Global Servants, a non-profit missions organization he founded in 1977.

The trustees honored Rutland for the legacy he left of balanced budgets, a new student center, $50 million in campus improvements, and increased enrollments.

Once more, the board was involved in a national search to recruit the university's fourth president.

6

UNITING CHARACTER AND CHARISMA

O ral Roberts had established ORU as a Charismatic university, but the new leadership wrestled with these questions:

- What does the Holy Spirit mean to today's generation?
- How do we communicate with millennials who are turned off by words such as "Charismatic" and "Pentecostal"?
- Are millennials acquainted with the Holy Spirit of Acts 2?

After much discussion, the Board of Trustees sponsored an initiative in partnership with the International Center for Spiritual Renewal called the "Commission on the Holy Spirit in the 21st Century."

Leading this effort was the Vice Chair of the Trustees, Dr. Billy Wilson. He announced that a major event would take place on the campus of ORU in April 2010, titled "Empowered21: Global Congress on Holy Spirit Empowerment in the 21st Century."

The idea for the conference came during a meeting of approximately 30 religious leaders in Orange County, California. Said Wilson, "Oral Roberts was present during that first conversation and was pleased with the concept of a global gathering linking the generations. He was thrilled with the idea that we would be putting energy and resources into connecting the next generation with the power of the Holy Spirit." Wilson observed, "This was the kind of big idea that Oral had for many years, so we felt like we were continuing with that tradition."

When Dr. Wilson announced the conference at a chapel service, he told the students, "I believe we are called to be the most dynamic, missional generation in the history of the world." Furthermore, "ORU should be the place where character and charisma unite and we become strong in our witness and empowered in a fresh way to reach the nations." He added, "We're inviting the world here next year to engage with us in seeking God for a fresh empowering of the Holy Spirit."

It had been more than 100 years since the Azusa Street Revival in Los Angeles, and the movement had grown to a global force of over 650 million people. But many students at ORU admitted that there was a definite gap between the language of their parents' era with the Charismatic renewal and young people today.

Leading up to this event, three avenues of conversation and preparation took place:

1. A leadership track—including leaders from the traditional Pentecostal and Charismatic communities as well as those from new, emerging ministries.
2. A scholars' track—with leading Pentecostal and Charismatic scholars and an intentional focus on diversity to facilitate a broad range of thought.
3. A next-generation track—a combination of contemporary ministry leaders and students to reflect on Spirit-empowered living today.

More than 500 leaders, scholars, and students, representing a wide variety of backgrounds, ages, and denominations, participated in 17 pre-conference conversation events on five continents.

The event far exceeded expectations. Over 9,000 attendees from 90 nations were represented and 210 educational sessions were offered during the conference. Plus, 35 scholarly papers were introduced for discussion on a variety of thought-provoking topics.

As the congress opened, invocations were given in nine different languages: Arabic, English, German, Greek, Hebrew,

Latin, Mandarin, Spanish, and Swahili.

Guest speakers included Jentezen Franklin, senior pastor of Free Chapel, Gainesville, Georgia; Ron Luce, president of Teen Mania Ministries; and Jack Hayford, founding pastor of The Church on The Way in Van Nuys, California.

The third evening featured speakers representing the seven continents of the world: E.A. Adeboye, Africa; Arthur Blessitt, Antarctica; Niko Njotorahardjo, Asia; Margaret Court, Australia; Ulf Ekman, Europe; Tommy Barnett, North America; and Claudio Freidzon, South America. The conference closed with an anointing service in which all of the attendees had the opportunity to be anointed with oil and prayed for by one of the various speakers or a member of the ministry team.

Said Wilson, "The conference was a reminder of the earth-shaking power of the Holy Spirit, a means of injecting new life into the vocabulary of the Holy Spirit, and a revisiting of the historic foundations of the Charismatic/Pentecostal movement."

There was a deliberate involvement of young voices at this historic gathering, and it left an indelible imprint on ORU. One attendee remarked, "I was encouraged to witness a purposeful passing of the 'Spirit-filled baton' to the next generation."

A NEW SEARCH AT A NEW ORU

The question of whether ORU would remain anchored to the vision of its founder was settled in many ways—by the backgrounds of the new Board of Trustees, by its revised constitution and bylaws, by its Spirit-led chapel services, and by the Global Congress on Holy Spirit Empowerment in the 21st Century.

With the resignation of Mark Rutland, the trustees faced its next challenge—finding a new president who would meet the requirements so unique to ORU. While Rutland's tenure was rather short, it was exactly what the university needed during a critical period of transition.

It was now time to find a qualified individual who had the potential to be a long-term president and lead the university in the years ahead.

At the April 2012 board meeting, a Presidential Search Committee was formed, chaired by Mart Green. The agenda for discussing the primary issues for the selection were:

- Vision with vitality
- Past performance
- Growth potential
- Funding
- ORU's diversity

The noted firm of CarterBaldwin Executive Search in Atlanta was retained to assist in the process. They had found leadership for many Fortune 500 companies, and had assisted Christian colleges including Wheaton, Pepperdine, and Liberty University School of Law.

When the official search notice was posted, the names of 170 potential candidates were submitted. By October, the pool was reduced to those the committee would personally interview.

Following the intensive search, the final name presented to the trustees was Dr. William "Billy" M. Wilson—the same individual who had served as Vice-Chair of the Board of Trustees for the previous four years, and the man who had led the highly successful "Empowered21: Global Congress on Holy Spirit Empowerment in the 21st Century."

His background and credentials were a perfect fit:

- Since 2005, he was the Executive Director of the International Center for Spiritual Renewal (ICSR), a parachurch non-profit interdenominational ministry. It led the Azuza Street Centennial in 2006 with 50,000 people from 112 nations in Los Angeles to celebrate the birth of the modern Pentecostal/ Charismatic movement.
- Co-chair of the Global Council and Executive Director of Empowered21.
- Launched Awakening America Alliance in 2008 and served as Chair of its Executive Cabinet. The Alliance

is the revival/renewal partner of Lausanne USA (Mission America Coalition).

- Host of "World Impact with Billy Wilson," the weekly television program of ICSR seen in 170 nations and heard in five different languages—celebrating 15 years on the air.
- Executive Producer (1994-2008) of Voice of Salvation Ministries, the award-winning communications arm of the Church of God of Prophecy denomination.
- Held several positions with the Church of God of Prophecy, including: Director of Kentucky State Youth Ministries (1979-83), Senior Pastor, Willard, Ohio (1983), International Director of Youth (1983-94), Director of Evangelism (1994-98), and Pastor of Peerless Road Church in Cleveland, Tennessee (1998-2003).
- Served as coordinator of the Cooperative Initiative for Evangelism between the Church of God and the Church of God of Prophecy (while recognized in both movements as an ordained bishop).

After earning a Bachelor of Science degree from Western Kentucky University, he received a Master of Arts in Church Ministries, Evangelism/World Missions from the Church of God Theological Seminary and Doctor of Ministry from the

ATS-accredited Pentecostal Theological Seminary, Cleveland, Tennessee.

Wilson also served on many advisory boards, including the International Christian Embassy Jerusalem and the Pentecostal World Fellowship. In addition, he was a member of the Board of Trustees of The National Interfaith Cable Coalition (Faith & Values Media), encompassing more than 200,000 congregations with 120 million congregants. This was a unique honor since he was the only Pentecostal and one of the few Evangelical voices in the entire membership.

In addition Wilson had authored several books, produced numerous video series, contributed to various publications, and lectured at international colleges, seminars, and conferences. Wilson was also an ordained bishop in the Church of God, Cleveland, Tennessee.

Also noteworthy was the fact that he and his wife, Lisa, were the parents of two children involved in full-time ministry.

STRATEGIES FOR GLOBALIZATION

The announcement of Wilson as ORU's fourth president was made January 31, 2013, and he began his official duties four months later.

From his first days in office, it was clear that Dr. Wilson

reflected a theme that had been a hallmark of ORU since Oral Roberts uttered the words, "Make no little plans here."

In addition, with "home base" becoming more stable and secure, he was able to lift the banner of Robert's original mandate from above: "Raise up your students to hear My voice, to go where My light is dim, where My voice is heard small, and My healing power is not known, even to the uttermost bounds of the earth."

Wilson told the trustees, "I believe ORU must move toward becoming a true global university. Strategies for this should include international partnerships for residential programs in other nations, the increase in online learning offerings, international worldwide learning opportunities for students from the Tulsa campus, and increased recruitment of overseas students to ORU, with those who excel in the whole person student profile."

The new president also stated, "The globalization of ORU will not be an easy process, nor will it be accomplished immediately. A several-year strategic plan needs to be thought through and implemented over time. But we must get started now."

"Getting started" didn't take Wilson long!

7

AN AMBITIOUS GOAL

The presidency of ORU was not a position that Wilson sought, but once nominated, he agreed to pray about the offer. "I wanted to make sure this was of God," he said. During this period of prayer, a number of things—providential, prophetic, and otherwise—led he and his wife, Lisa, to believe that it indeed was God's will.

Dr. Wilson's worldview and his vision for ORU were reflected in his first official act on the day he took office, June 1, 2013. He appointed a "Presidential Task Force on the Globalization of ORU." This was a group of stellar international leaders from inside and outside the university.

This think tank would brainstorm ORU's future and consider questions such as where our world is headed, what is happening in higher education, and how ORU can accomplish its mission in today's culture.

The Task Force recognized the explosion of interest in

education taking place around the globe, and that hundreds of thousands of international students were currently studying in America—280,000 Chinese alone. In addition, millions were taking online courses from every corner of the earth.

One of the outcomes of the Task Force was a Case Statement for the globalization of the university, which was unanimously affirmed at the Fall 2013 meeting of the Board of Trustees.

The document included creating a stronger global culture on the Tulsa campus, increasing opportunities through online learning and technology, and a commitment to ultimately expanding ORU's presence to every inhabited continent.

The Case Statement included these conclusions:

- "The market demand for education has never been higher than in today's knowledge-based economy. The need for professional training is astronomically high around the world, and the majority of the world is becoming able to pay at some level for high quality education. Partnerships and technological means are now available to address the growing need."

- "The global economy has become the new world order. Millionaires and billionaires are being pro-duced from the creation of international markets. From software engineers to electronic app developers, technology is creating its own rich among ordinary people. These men and women need knowledge to thrive in the knowledge-based economy. They are willing to pay, at least to some degree, for an education that connects knowledge and its application. The whole person education 'invented' at ORU with its unique characteristics and applications will be of great value to the world, expecially the Spirit-empowered segment of the Christian world."

- "The spiritual genius of the founder of Oral Roberts University is seen clearly in the whole person educational philosophy of the university. This institution was built on the authority of the Holy Spirit to develop whole persons to go where God's light is seen dim, His voice is heard small, and His healing power is not known. Oral Roberts used the most advanced technology of his day to fulfill ORU's mission. The university was well known for its state-of-the-art educational technology. Globalization is inherent in ORU's mission. The time has come for ORU to recapture its original vision, use the innovative technology of this generation, and fulfill its mission in the globalized world of the 21st century."

An early result of the Task Force was the forming of an academic partnership with Asia Life University (ALU) in Daejeon, South Korea. Students enrolled in what was called "The 1-Plus-3 Program" study at ALU for one year. After completing up to 30 hours of undergraduate course credits at the South Korea university, students with adequate Test of English as a Foreign Language scores would have the opportunity to study in Tulsa for the remaining three years and receive a bachelor's degree from ORU. Students in the program could apply for the Quest Whole Person Scholarship and other financial awards.

"EAGLE DAY"

For the sixth summer in a row, and during Dr. Wilson's first summer as president, several major deferred mainte-nance projects were underway, including new systems to lower energy costs, Information Technology upgrades, new sidewalks, and the repaving of parking lots.

What the freshmen and returning students liked most when they arrived in August were several new food options and that more than 500 extra-long mattresses were already in the dorms, with more planned.

That fall, ORU had another increase in enrollment but

they certainly didn't expect that an event at one of the early chapel services after Wilson became president would be featured on *The Today Show, Good Morning America, Fox News,* and more than 90 million internet video downloads.

It started when Dr. Wilson thought it would be great to have what they called "Eagle Day"—to reflect on what it means to be a Golden Eagle at ORU, along with the Bible's challenge to live like an eagle.

They contacted the Wild Bird Sanctuary near St. Louis and arranged to have Kili, a live golden eagle, brought to campus for a special demonstration. Joining Kili was a bald eagle named Lewis who performs at events such as St. Louis Cardinals baseball games.

As Dr. Wilson describes the scene, "Chapel was going well. Kili came on stage as I spoke on 'Living like an Eagle.' Midway through my message, we planned to have Lewis fly from the balcony to the stage...this was practiced beforehand with Roger the trainer, and we knew exactly where to stand and what to do."

Lewis appeared in the balcony, and everyone turned to watch his flight. But instead of performing as planned, the bald eagle, for whatever reason, made an unexpected turn and headed straight for a window, slamming into the glass at full speed and crashing to the floor.

Wilson recalls, "I watched in horror as the situation

unfolded and was thinking, 'I have killed a bald eagle to start my presidency. Great job. It probably won't be a long presidency!'"

Then, to everyone's relief, Roger, the trainer, coaxed Lewis onto his arm and brought him to the stage for the conclusion of the service.

Several students had their phones out and captured the crash on video. One video was posted on YouTube and it went viral very quickly.

The result was one of the largest PR moments in ORU history.

AN INVITATION TO THE WORLD

The inauguration ceremony of Dr. William "Billy" Wilson on September 20, 2013, reflected ORU's commitment to globalization. It began with a processional of the university's faculty members, trustees, and dignitaries from other Christian universities. Then came a "Parade of Nations," with students carrying flags of 193 countries, many held by natives of that land, dressed in ethnic attire. This wasn't difficult to arrange since the ORU student body comprised of men and women from 80 nations.

Board Chair Mart Green welcomed students, alumni, faculty, staff, friends, university representatives, and government dignitaries by saying, "We want to invite the entire world to ORU."

Dr. Edward O. Blews, Jr., then-President of the Council for Christian Colleges and Universities, described Wilson as "a passionate global influencer" and remarked, "Today marks a marvelous match made in heaven between a terrific leader in President Wilson and a tremendous university...for the great benefit of this community and world."

The impressive ceremony included prayers of investiture in several foreign languages and greetings from Christian leaders worldwide, both in person and by video.

As Wilson began his address, there were images of major foreign cities flashing on a huge video screen behind him. He cast his vision for a global ORU, reminding that the mission was firmly set by the university's founder and first president, Oral Roberts. Said Wilson, "Forty-eight years ago, ORU was a United States university with an outreach to the nations. In the 21st century we must become a global university whose main campus happens to be in the center of the United States."

Wilson believes ORU is perfectly positioned in a changing world to become a global institution—"a place where people from every nation can come. In the nearly half-century since ORU was founded, our planet has become a different place...a global community."

He also pointed out how higher learning has expanded

dramatically, with the demand for knowledge exploding. "Millions of people are entering the middle class for the first time and have an opportunity to pursue a higher education," he observed. Many of them are involved in what he calls the "Spirit-empowered" movement.

Noting that the Pentecostal/Charismatic movement has become the fastest-growing arm of Christianity here and abroad, this was his message to them: "We are here to serve you. ORU is for you, and we must never lose its original vision to prepare students to take the message of Christ to the world."

FROM EVERYWHERE TO EVERYWHERE

Regarding globalization, Wilson believes, "The missions paradigm has changed. Now, people are sent *from* everywhere *to* everywhere. We believe God is calling ORU to intersect what the Holy Spirit is doing around the world and help build leaders that are Spirit-empowered to bring God's healing to our generation *from* everywhere *to* everywhere."

The vision of Empowered21, as explained by Wilson, is "that every person on earth would have an authentic encounter with Jesus Christ through the power and presence of the Holy Spirit by Pentecost 2033."

This is an ambitious goal, but he believes it fits with ORU's mission statement. He also is convinced that "vision brings provision," and donors will invest to see this become reality.

From his first days in office, Wilson expressed that he was under no pretense that he can accomplish all the goals himself. "We need the collective wisdom, the collective understanding, even the collective inspiration of the ORU family."

This was a vision that would result in unexpected miracles in the days ahead.

8

THE FIVE-YEAR ADAPTIVE PLAN

A major milestone in the history of ORU was fast approaching for the university that commenced in 1965—the 50th anniversary.

"We knew this was a time for a renewed commitment to the historic mission," said President Wilson, "but we needed to move from *sustaining* the institution to renewing, growing, and expanding its vision."

The Globalization Task Force, appointed by President Wilson on his first day in office in the summer of 2013, took their charge seriously. They studied the problems and possibilities that were awaiting the revitalized ORU.

After an in-depth analysis that lasted several months, the task force, which consisted of representatives from all ORU constituencies, produced a list of specific propositions. These were reviewed and ranked by the Board of Trustees and three were adopted as top priorities:

1. Creation of a global culture that will drive the ORU identity of Whole Person Education.
2. Attention to the development of an integrated Whole Person Education learning system that physically and functionally assists with the transformation of global learners.
3. Reshaping ORU's business plan to reflect institutional excellence with economic sustainability.

Once these were established, the board called on the University Planning Council (UPC) to develop a plan to implement these priorities over the next five years.

The UPC was designed as "a shared governance council designed to facilitate collaboration between faculty, administration and the Board of Trustees with an equal number of representatives from each group." The UPC committed its work to developing "a mission-based, futuristic, and robust plan that has the capacity for adaptive course correction, campus-wide buy-in, and motivational momentum."

Wilson noted that the plan was developed with prayer, faith, and hope, and in a context of dynamic exchange on hard questions. "Intentional efforts were made to create goals and objectives that are realistic, action-oriented, measurable, and with considered input from all who are affected by its directives," said the president.

The Plan

The final document of the UPC was approved by the board in March 2015 and "An Adaptive Five-Year Plan for Oral Roberts University" was formally announced.

The goals and objectives were clear:

1. Expand Access Throughout the World to Spirit-Empowered Whole Person Education

- Enroll 7,500 students per year with 5,000 students in credit and 2,500 students in non-credit educational programs
- Connect a worldwide audience to ORU educational opportunities
- Establish a Tulsa-based global learning and technology center
- Demonstrate that 100% of all faculty have received training to participate in ORU virtual learning communities
- Establish collaborative access partnerships to develop learning communities on every inhabited continent
- Increase the number of international students by 1,000

- Increase the number of countries represented in the student body to 100

2. Create a Thriving Global Culture Within the University

- Demonstrate that the International Center regularly interacts with international students to assist in cultural adjustment, academic progress, and spiritual growth
- Host at least two international cultural events for the entire Tulsa campus community each year
- Increase the number of international staff and faculty
- Develop academic programs and services to improve the experience of English as a Foreign Language (EFL) students
- Provide global cultural competency training and development opportunities to 100% of faculty and fulltime staff
- Increase the percentage of graduating students who have participated in an intercultural experience to 100%

3. Improve the Quality and Value of the Academic Education Received by ORU Students

- Increase engagement in learning, research, and relevant inquiry
- Integrate real-life learning opportunities (e.g., internships) into the academic experience of 75% of graduating students
- Increase the number of faculty with terminal degrees to 70%
- Increase by 25% the number of students who engage in research, publish in peer-reviewed publications, or present to audiences outside of ORU
- Have distinguished faculty members in each college recognized for their scholarship at an international level
- Increase ORU's graduation rate by 15%

4. Adapt Quickly to Opportunities and Challenges while Maintaining Mission and Purpose

- Empower staff to resolve most constituent concerns to satisfaction without needing to obtain multiple approvals
- Streamline university policies and procedures
- Increase lines of communication through a variety of interactive formats
- Implement continuous service improvement through training of staff

- Create a multi-disciplinary team to quarterly analyze global issues and opportunities and make recommendations
- Implement continuous evaluation and improvement processes for programs, curricula, and faculty

5. *Serve the Global Spirit-Empowered Movement as ORU's Primary Constituency*

- Develop and implement ten new certificate programs to support the Spirit-empowered movement
- Establish 500 partnerships and ministerial/institutional alliances in the Spirit-empowered movement
- Establish an advisory group of Spirit-empowered leaders on how ORU can best serve their constituencies
- Provide global access to the Holy Spirit Research Center
- Have each college engage in at least one professional, educational, or research project specifically designed to address a need in the Spirit-empowered movement

6. *Teach and Demonstrate the Healing Power of Jesus Christ*

- Incorporate the founding vision and history of ORU into new student, faculty, and staff orientations
- Create a new general education, multi-disciplinary course specifically focused on healing
- Create and send 150 short-term mission teams throughout the world
- Develop five multi-disciplinary, incarnational healing development projects to transform communities for the glory of Jesus Christ

7. Enhance Economic Sustainability Leading to Financial Vitality

- Increase development revenue raised from outside sources—donations, grants, endowments, other donations, etc.—by $100 million
- Increase auxiliary revenues by 20%
- Increase the participation of alumni and friends in University initiatives and giving by 20%
- Establish economic stability and market viability of academic programming
- Increase global marketing efforts by 30%

8. *Strive to Become the Premier Spirit-Empowered University*

- Produce Spirit-empowered thought-leaders, consultants, speakers, and problem-solvers in and across multiple disciplines
- Increase the number and/or level of accredited academic programs
- Establish at least one Ph.D. program
- Increase engagement with Spirit-empowered organizations and events worldwide
- Launch a comprehensive global public communication strategy to strengthen awareness of ORU

POSITIONING FOR THE FUTURE

The five-year adaptive plan was designed to be assessed annually by the UPC and utilized in directing the Board of Trustees, administration, and faculty in making effective decisions for the continued pursuit of God's vision for the institution. Said Wilson, "We believe this will properly position the university for the next 50 years and increase its potential to become the premier Spirit-empowered university."

Speaking of the future, Wilson predicted, "Fifty years from

now, higher education will be exceptionally different than it is today. Technology, mobility, opportunity, and the increase of knowledge will all affect higher education dramatically. Some universities will not make it through these changes, but I am confident that ORU will not only survive but thrive."

THE COMPREHENSIVE CAMPAIGN

During this time the university announced a $50 million fund raising project: "The 50th Anniversary Comprehensive Campaign—To the Uttermost Bounds of the Earth."

There were four major components:

1. Globalization of Whole Person Education: $18 million
2. Enhanced Physical Campus: $14 million
3. Quest Whole Person Scholarships: $18 million
    In addition to this $50 million, there was one more:
4. Strengthen University Endowment: $20 million

President Wilson and the development office made a strong case to donors: "ORU has no long-term debt. The recent fiscal year closed in the black without utilizing any lines of credit. More than $100 million has been infused into campus revitalization since 2008. Enrollment has risen every year since 2009. The time to expand is now."

CONSISTENT BOARD LEADERSHIP

Mart Green served as Chair of the Board of Trustees for the first six years of the "New ORU," but at the April 2014 board meeting, the trustees, in keeping with bylaws, chose a new chair—and from that point forward would have periodic changes in chair leadership. Their unanimous choice was Rob Hoskins (with Green named as vice-chair).

Hoskins is President and CEO of OneHope, a Florida-based global ministry committed to engaging every child in the world with God's Word. The organization has reached more than a billion children and youth in more than 140 nations and in 100+ languages.

President Wilson commended the board for their choice, noting that "Rob, who successfully leads a very substantial and effective global ministry, has a deep understanding of the opportunities for the globalization of ORU into the future."

That future was *now*—because the university was about to enter a memorable year.

9

A YEAR OF JUBILEE

It was a time for celebration! August 2015 marked the 50th year since ORU's first freshman class stepped foot on the brand new campus. Now, a half-century later, more than 40,000 alumni were serving in 130 different countries.

Special events were scheduled over a multi-year period, culminating with the 50th graduating class.

During the third week of October 2015, dozens of activities took place—academic lectures, a fall festival, departmental showcases, sporting events, concerts, class reunions, receptions, even a 50th anniversary parade and fireworks!

More than 1,200 attended a sold-out gala in the Grand Ballroom of Tulsa's Renaissance Hotel. Grammy award-winner Sandi Patti was the guest soloist and the featured speakers were Will Graham, grandson of Billy Graham, and Gigi Graham, the evangelist's daughter. Their presence brought memories of Billy Graham's address at the dedication of ORU. Some could remember hearing him say, "Here at Oral Roberts University, these young people are being taught not only how to make a living, but how to live."

CONTRIBUTORS TO ORU'S HISTORY

This was also a time to honor individuals and organizations who had made a significant impact on ORU— and on the world—in positive ways as an extension of the university and its mission. This led to the selection of 50 men and women who received "The ORU 50th Anniversary Lifetime Global Achievement Awards."

The names of these honorees are well worth mentioning because of their contributions to the history of the university:

Seth Ablorh – '85 M.D. Returned to Ghana to establish a hospital and mission.

Daniel Amen – '85 M.D. Noted psychiatrist and author.

Michele Bachmann – '86 J.D. Elected to the U.S. House of Representatives (served 2007-2015).

Andretti Bain – '07, '09 MBA. ORU track record holder and Olympic medalist from the Bahamas.

S. Lee Braxon (posthumous) – Founding Chairman of ORU Board of Regents.

James Buskirk – Founding Dean of ORU's School of Theology (1976-1984).

Amick Byram – '77. Recording artist and two-time Grammy nominee.

Cardone Family – Automotive parts manufacturer Michael Cardone, Sr., was an early supporter of ORU. His son, Michael, Jr. ('70), daughter-in-law Jacqueline ('69), and grandson, Michael III ('96), have served on the Board of Trustees.

Delta Cavner – '72. Fulbright Award recipient, and tenured faculty member of Southwest Baptist University.

Matthews Chacko – '70. Founded the 900-student Bethany Academy in India and opened the only evangelical Christian TV station in India, serving 50 million people.

Don Colbert – '80, '84 M.D. Board-certified family practice physician in Central Florida. He has authored more than 40 bestselling health books.

Phil Cooke – '76. Writer and speaker who has produced media programming in nearly 50 countries.

Kenneth Cooper – Noted pioneer of preventive medicine who inspired Oral Roberts to add aerobics to the university's curriculum.

Daugherty Family – Billy Joe ('74, '92 M.A., '02 D.Min) and wife Sharon ('76) founded Tulsa's Victory Christian Center. He served as ORU's interim president before his passing.

Bernis Duke – Spent 33 years as ORU's men's tennis coach, and was inducted into Intercollegiate Tennis Association Hall of Fame.

Ralph and Darlene Fagin – Dr. Fagin ('70) served ORU for 40 years on the faculty, administration, and as an interim president. His wife Darlene ('76) served the university in various capacities.

Richard Fenimore – '77, '79 MBA. President and Co-Founder of Trinity Chemical Industries, Tulsa.

Richard Fuqua – '74. Three time ORU Basketball All-American, averaging 27 points per game. Drafted by NBA's Boston Celtics.

Kathie Lee Gifford – Former ORU student who spent 15 years co-hosting the television show, "Regis and Kathy Lee." Currently with NBC-TV.

Mart Green – Serves as Board Chair of family-owned Hobby Lobby. Founding Chair of ORU's new Board of Trustees.

Carl Hamilton – The university's Chief Academic Officer for almost 30 years.

Marilyn Hickey – host of a television ministry since 1973 and the longest-tenured member of ORU's original Board of Regents.

Scott Howard – '70. President of Commercial Roofers in Nevada and served on the Board of Trustees.

In His Image – A Christian family medicine residency
program that considers itself an offshoot of ORU.
It has served 16,000 patients.

Bill Kuert – '68 M.Div. Missionary and educator in
Kenya since 1978.

Terry Law – '69. Founder of World Compassion. Author
of "The Story of Jesus," which has sold over 27
million copies worldwide in 52 languages.

Dennis Lindsay – '04 M.A, '14 D.Min. CEO of Christ for
the Nations, an international missions organization.

Madeline Manning Mims – '11 M.Div. Member of four
U.S. Olympic Teams and the only American woman
ever to win gold in the 800 meters.

Stephen Mansfield – '81. Speaker and author of *New
York Times* bestsellers including *The Faith of
George W. Bush.*

J. D. McKean – Medical doctor who established the
JDM Foundation, which has provided scholarships to
hundreds of ORU students.

John and Ruth Merrell – Both members of ORU's first
class. Missionaries who have served 35 years in
many nations.

Don Moen – Singer, songwriter, and Dove Award-
winning producer of worship music. The former
student became president of Integrity Music.

Mike Moore – A 1981 Baseball All-American at ORU. Drafted by the Seattle Mariners and spent 16 years in the major leagues.

Larry Wayne Morbitt – '74. Singer, actor, who played the role of Ubaldo Piangi in *The Phantom of the Opera* on Broadway for eight years. Plus, he has has spent 15 years as a minister of music in various churches.

Myles Munroe (posthumous) – '78. Founded Bahamas Faith Ministries. Received British Empire Award for his spiritual and social contributions to the Bahamas.

David Osborne – '81. Known as "Pianist to the Presidents," having played at the White House for Presidents Carter, Bush (George H. W.), Reagan, and Clinton.

Paul Osteen – '78, '82 M.D. Spent 17 years as a surgeon before joining the pastoral team of Joel Osteen, his brother, at Lakewood Church in Houston, Texas.

Winnie Perdue – Popular employee at the City of Faith and ORU's Alumni Relations Office. Great-great-granddaughter of the famous Cherokee, Sequoyah.

Cindy Perry – '74. Founded Himalayan Ministries and was appointed South Asia regional director for Development Associates International.

Laura Pratt Nelson – '88 MSN. Medical missionary based in Oaxaca, Mexico who has ministered to over 80,000 patients.

Ruth Rooks – Volunteered at age 15 to type letters for Oral Roberts. She became his only secretary for his entire life and ministry.

Robert Stamps – A chaplain at ORU for 13 years, he established the summer missions program.

Larry Stockstill – '75. Founded Bethany World Prayer Center in Louisiana. The ministry has planted over 22,000 churches in more than 35 nations.

Jim Stovall – '81. President of Emmy Award-winning Narrative Television Network. Author of *The Ultimate Gift,* which became a major motion picture.

Clifton Taulbert – '71. Born in the segregated Mississippi Delta, he became the first African-American to win the Mississippi Institute of Arts and Letters Award for Nonfiction Writing.

Ted Timmermans – '78. Chief Accounting Officer for Tulsa-based Williams Partners GP, LLC.

Ken Trickey (posthumous) – ORU's men's head basketball coach (1969-1974). His teams won more games than any other team in the nation except UCLA.

Frank Wallace – Architect and designer of the future-focused ORU campus.

Pansy Wallace – Served ORU students for over 40 years in several capacities. Her kind words and love for students made her a favorite staff member.

Kelly Wright – '08. Television reporter and anchor for Fox News Channel.

A PERSONAL JUBILEE

During an anniversary week chapel service, Dr. Wilson focused on the fact that Scripture is filled with instructions for feasts and moments of commemoration. He said, "Divinely instituted times of celebration were important to the people of God as they remembered their blessings and recommitted to their mission."

He also reminded those gathered that one unique observance took place every 50th year (Leviticus 25). It was when debts were forgiven, slaves were set free, and the fields were allowed to rest. "Jubilee was a time of restoration, renewal, release, and huge celebration!"

A significant moment that morning was when Wilson announced the names of ten ORU students whose college debts up to $2,500 were being forgiven (and if they had no debts, they now had an account on which they could draw).

The university randomly selected the students through a drawing and it was symbolic of what took place in Bible days. Those whose names were called had the joy of a personal Jubilee!

By the Numbers

Wilson was thrilled with the university's progress during the 50th anniversary year: "We more than doubled our online degree offerings, increased the number of undergraduate programs from 64 to 77, launched plans for a new Ph.D. program in Theology for Global Christian Studies as well as a Doctorate of Nursing Practice—and we saw another spike in enrollment." Plus, the university celebrated the largest, most successful capital campaign in its history.

ORU has always attracted foreign students, but in the fall of 2015, an International Center was established with these objectives:

1. To create diverse cultural experiences across campus
2. To assist all students with becoming cross-culturally competent
3. To help international students with cultural, academic, and spiritual integration and growth

The Center, located on the first floor of Claudius Priscilla Roberts Hall, has become a welcoming and caring environment, providing needed support for students, staff, and faculty in regards to ORU's global reach and mission. It also partners with Admissions to strengthen international recruiting efforts.

A HEALTHY STUDENT BODY

Since its founding, the university has taken seriously the Whole Person philosophy of body, mind, and spirit. Regarding the physical self, students have always been required to participate in health and fitness activities and turn in a written record which impacts their grades. Starting in 2015, the emphasis reached a higher level. Now, incoming freshmen and transfer students are given a Fitbit—a stylish electronic wristband that measures an individual's steps and heart rate.

This data is transferred directly into a computer program that interfaces with ORU's grading system. The goal is 10,000 steps per day and 150 minutes each week of exercise that produces an elevated heart rate.

Since all undergrads are required to take a physical fitness course each semester, the marriage of technology with the school's health objectives was natural.

This cutting-edge program garnered the university national and international attention.

NEW LEADERSHIP

A highly-qualified administrative team was now in place. It included Dr. Kathaleen Reid-Martinez as the new Provost and Chief Academic Officer. She came to ORU with an extensive background in educational leadership and online learning at some of America's premier Christian universities and graduate schools.

Dr. Wilson was also pleased to announce the appointment of Neal Stenzel as Chief Financial Officer of the university. After graduating from ORU in 1988 and earning the CPA designation, he worked for the "Big Four" accounting firm of Ernst and Young for three years before being named to positions of Controller and CFO at several large corporations.

The new leadership team also included Michael Mathews as Associate Vice President of Technology and Innovation. His credentials include more than 24 years of experience as a senior-level information technology executive. Mathews holds a graduate degree from UCLA and specialized certificates from several institutions including the Harvard Business School. "Mike has the depth of experience we need to have excellence in IT to be highly effective in the global marketplace," noted President Wilson.

During the 50th anniversary year, with the worldwide footprint of ORU spreading far and wide, Ossie Mills, a 1983 graduate, was named Vice President of Global Communications and Marketing. Mills, who has a stellar background in international media, was also appointed Executive Director of Empowered21 and leader of university-owned GEB America Television Network.

Under Mills's direction, GEB America has experienced record growth. It was launched by Oral Roberts in 1966 as a Tulsa television station, eventually being added to DirectTV.

The program schedule includes many prominent ministries, plus chapel services from ORU, live university sports, and "World Impact with Dr. Billy Wilson."

The network has a potential audience of more than 34 million. In 2016, GEB began broadcasting in the San Francisco Bay Area and has added other cities including Orlando, Florida. The university's network can be seen on Apple TV and viewed online at *gebamerica.com* and by downloading the free GEB America App.

ON TO JERUSALEM

The entire anniversary year saw ORU involved in multiple events, perhaps none more epic than what took place thousands of miles from campus—the 2015 Empowered21 Global Conference in Jerusalem.

More than 4,500 people from 70 nations gathered to celebrate Pentecost in the Land of Pentecost for five days in May. Night after night, thousands packed Jerusalem's Pais Arena and the services were streamed live on the internet. A surprisingly large number of attendees were from Asia —mainly from Indonesia and China.

The co-chairs for this historic event were Dr. Wilson from ORU and Dr. George Wood, General Superintendent of the Assemblies of God.

The speakers list included a "who's who" of the Pentecostal/Charismatic world: Reinhard Bonnke, founder of Christ For All Nations, Claudio Freidzon, pastor of the 20,000-member Rey de Reys Church in Argentina, Prince Guneratnam (Malaysia), Chairman of Pentecostal World Fellowship, Mark Williams, General Overseer of the Church of God—and 130 more international leaders.

100+ ORU students made the journey, serving the attendees, basking in the spiritual awakening, and personally ministering in the Holy Land. They were divided into 12 mission teams—named after the tribes of Israel. Their ministry also included the practical. For example, some gave haircuts and manicures in local communities, while others cleaned streets and painted buildings.

Instead of being a showcase for world-class speakers, the

delegates were spiritually challenged to return to their respective countries and impact the culture.

A highlight was the Pentecost Unity Celebration and Baptism Service at the Jordan River—held at the spot where it is believed Jesus was baptized by John the Baptist.

Steve Strang, publisher of *Charisma Magazine,* wrote, "I've been to many large Pentecostal Gatherings over the years—probably an average of one a year for 40 years. This one had a good spirit. No big egos were evident. Powerful ministry took place. Despite the doom and gloom we often hear, there seemed to be optimism about the work of the Holy Spirit around the world. If anything, the message seemed to be that, with the world we live in, we have no choice but to rely on the power of the Holy Spirit."

"It was a large undertaking," said ORU's Ossie Mills, "but we believe the event was a stepping stone for the continued explosion of the work of the Holy Spirit around this planet."

THE THREE NAPKINS

In the summer of 2015, President Wilson returned to Beijing to pursue a number of initiatives for expanding ORU's reach into the world's most populous nation, China. During a breakfast meeting with a Chinese businessman and his wife, his thoughts raced back to his inaugural address at becoming president of the university two years earlier. A subset theme of his message was what he called "A Tale of Three Napkins."

The first was the vision Oral Roberts received while having dinner with Pat Robertson in the summer of 1960. Roberts reached for a table napkin and wrote down the commission the Lord gave him that day, which we have referred to earlier—to "raise up your students to hear My voice, to go where My light is dim, where My voice is heard small, and My healing power is not known, even to the uttermost bounds of the earth. Their work will exceed yours, and in this I am well pleased."

The second napkin he mentioned was when Jesus rose from the dead after the crucifixion. In the garden tomb, He took time to fold the cloth (or napkin) that covered His head (John 20:7), signifying that He would finish what He began. Applying the illustration to the university, Wilson stated that he firmly believed the Lord would complete what He envisioned for ORU back in 1960.

The third napkin involved a personal experience the president had during his first visit to China years earlier. He recounted, "We were having a meal with our Chinese tour guide, and I felt led to reach for a napkin as a makeshift tract, and write down the letters A, B, C." I explained to the woman, "These letters stand for 'Ask,' 'Believe,' and 'Confess'—I then gave her the plan of salvation." The Holy

Spirit was present; she accepted Christ and it was his first Chinese convert.

Now, several years later, Wilson was back in Beijing. Part of the local team included a Chinese businessman and his wife, who were helping to form key relationships for ORU. She was a recent convert, while he was not a believer.

"On my last day in China," recalls Wilson, "at breakfast, there were two paper napkins on the table and the Holy Spirit prompted me, 'Use your tract.'" So, in obedience, he turned toward the gentleman and asked, "Can I give you a quick English lesson?"

He politely agreed, and Wilson wrote A. B. C. on one of the napkins. God honored His Word once more and this led to the businessman receiving Jesus. "I still have a similar napkin laying on my desk from my inauguration, which serves as a constant reminder to me of the ever-present worldwide spiritual hunger."

STRONG FOOTING

Back in Oklahoma, when the students arrived on campus for the fall semester, it was another year of increasing enrollment. Most impressive was the fact that freshmen retention remained strong—at over 80 percent for the sixth consecutive year.

As a sign that the university was in good hands, President Wilson accepted a contract extension from the Board of Trustees through the summer of 2021. In the words of board chair Rob Hoskins, "We did a thorough review of Dr. Wilson's service over the past two years and have found it to be exemplary. He has built a strong pathway to the future that we want to see him carry through."

Hoskins added, "As a board, we are excited about the possibilities with the University under Dr. Wilson's care. We know that we are on strong footing to reach 'the uttermost bounds of the Earth.'"

As the Golden Anniversary drew to its conclusion, Dr. Wilson observed, "For 50 years, ORU has drawn future leaders from all over the world. In the next 50 years, ORU will build a truly global network of world-class, whole-person education opportunities—in Tulsa, and on every inhabited continent."

He remarked, "Our world needs ORU now more than it did 50 years ago, and we are ready for the challenge ahead."

10

WHAT'S IT
ALL ABOUT?

When outside observers speak of "The New ORU," the conversation usually centers on the financial turnaround, the physical improvements on campus, and new leadership. But that's only part of the story. To the Board of Trustees, faculty, alumni, and administration, it's all about the students!

- Oral Roberts's original commission from God was: "Raise up your <u>students</u> to hear My voice, to go where My light is dim..."
- The newly revised bylaws state: "The University is committed to assist <u>students</u> in their quest for knowledge of their personal relationship to God, to mankind, and to the universe in which we live."
- The mission statement of ORU includes the words:"...To build Holy Spirit-empowered leaders through <u>whole person</u> education to impact the world with God's healing."

As mentioned earlier, one of the first major announcements of the new Board of Trustees was to establish what is known as the Quest Whole Person Scholarship.

Since its inception, more than 5,000 students have received full or partial grants to ORU through the program—which attracts top young men and women from the U.S. and abroad.

The competition to receive these awards (which range in value of up to full tuition per year) increases annually, and the scholarships are renewable for up to four years.

Hundreds of high schools across the nation make the information available to their graduating seniors, and many guidance counselors promote the program.

Those selected from the nominees are invited to campus for Scholarship Day Competitions in the fall or spring and the recipients are selected by the Scholarship Review Committee. Interest has grown to the point that ORU now schedules five separate on-campus interview dates each year.

In addition to developing intellectually, emotionally, spiritually, physically, and professionally, students who receive these awards must demonstrate:

- A Christian worldview
- A lifestyle of service
- Academic achievement

- Leadership ability
- Vision to make a life-changing impact on others
- A healthy lifestyle

Students who reside outside of the United States and are invited to participate in a Quest Whole Person Scholarship Event can arrange for a phone interview in place of traveling to the campus.

Here is an example: Vonny Kumala of Indonesia wanted to study abroad—at ORU—but the cost appeared too high. "My dad told me to pray about it," she said. "I think it's amazing how God kept opening doors for me." A Quest scholarship was one of those doors. "To be able to go here, it is a miracle."

Laura Bishop, Vice President of Development and Alumni Relations pointed out, "Through Quest, we're recruiting the best and the brightest."

The program is maintained through the gifts of generous donors with a heart for education and a belief in the work of the university—and every donation is matched dollar-for-dollar.

THE HONOR CODE

ORU is not for everyone. Before a person considers

enrolling in the university, they are encouraged to read the Student Honor Code and decide if he or she feels comfortable living by its regulations.

At the beginning of each academic year, ORU students sign the Honor Code and pledge to follow all the standards listed.

The first paragraph begins, "In signing the Code of Honor I fully recognize that Oral Roberts University was founded to be and is committed to being a Christian religious ministry and that it offers a lifestyle of commitment to Jesus Christ of Nazareth as personal Savior and Lord and as an integral part of its evangelistic outreach. It is therefore my personal commitment to be a person of integrity in my attitude and respect for what Oral Roberts University is in its calling to be a Christian University."

The Code includes several specific pledges regarding applying themselves intellectually, spiritually, and physically for the glory of God. Plus, the students agree to attend required chapel services and abide by the rules and regulations that are adopted from time to time by the university.

There are two specific parts of the code that speak to social issues. They are as follows:

- I PLEDGE to cultivate good relationships socially with others and to seek to love others as I love myself. I

will not lie, I will not steal, I will not curse, I will not
be a talebearer. I will not cheat or plagiarize; I will
do my own academic work and will not inappropri-
ately collaborate with other students on assignments.

- I PLEDGE at all times to keep my total being under
  subjection from all immoral and illegal actions and
  communications, whether on or off campus. I will
  not take any illegal drugs or misuse any drugs. I will
  not engage in or attempt to engage in any illicit,
  unscriptural sexual acts, which include any homo-
  sexual activity and sexual intercourse with one who
  is not my spouse. I will not be united in marriage
  other than the marriage between one man and one
  woman. I will not drink alcoholic beverages of any
  kind; I will not use tobacco; I will not engage in
  other behavior that is contrary to the rules and regulations listed in the Student Handbook.

By signing the Code, the student acknowledges that ORU
is a private school and that he or she has no vested rights in
the governing of the school. They accept their attendance as
a *privilege* and *not* a right and that the University reserves
the authority to require the withdrawal of a student at any
time if, in the judgment of the president of the University or
of the ORU Disciplinary/Academic Grievance Committee,

such action is deemed necessary to safeguard ORU's ideals of scholarship or the spiritual and moral atmosphere of it as a Christian university.

The final paragraph of the document reads: "I will keep the Honor Code carefully and prayerfully. I understand that my signature below is my acceptance of the entire Code of Honor and completes a contract between me and Oral Roberts University which is a prerequisite for matriculation and becomes a part of my permanent file. Further, my acceptance of the Code of Honor is a solemn vow and promise to God as to how I will live my life."

ONE-ON-ONE

The greatest recruiters for ORU are the students themselves—and the Admissions Office plays to this strength. A fall and spring "College Weekend" brings hundreds of high school and transfer students from across the world to "test drive" college classes, explore scholarship opportunities, and find out what a Spirit-empowered campus is like. Prospective students can audition for Talent Scholarships if they're interested in majoring in art, dance, drama, broadcasting, or music.

When those who visit and apply to ORU are asked, "What impressed you most?" the answer frequently heard is,

"Staying in the dorm and making friends with some of the students."

Those who are unable to attend a major "College Weekend" can schedule an "Eagle Day" most weekdays when school is in session. They are assigned a "Student Ambassador" for a customized tour of campus, visit classes that are of interest, attend a Wednesday or Friday chapel service, and spend the night in a dorm.

There's also a special weekend event, "Graduate School Showcase," for those who want to explore either the Graduate School of Business, the Graduate School of Education, or the Graduate School of Theology & Ministry. It includes visiting classes, meeting faculty and deans, learning about academic and financial aid opportunities—and spending time with grad students already enrolled in the programs.

DIGITAL INTERACTION

ORU is constantly lauded and commended for embracing new technologies. For example, students enjoy a "digital concierge" platform, a cloud-based portal that organizes web-based campus services in one location—everything from email, events, athletics, counseling, maps, degree plan sheets, academic calendars, curriculum, and dining services. Its search tool allows quick connections with resources and services from any mobile device or computer.

But that's not all. By using ORU's "telepresence robots" (think of an 8-pound digital camera mounted on a Segway), prospective students can take campus tours, attend classes, and have their questions answered via live two-way audio and video streaming. As one user explained, "It's the closest thing to being on campus without actually being there."

Technology is also revolutionizing the classroom experience. For example, since becoming president, every year Dr. Wilson teaches a class called "Spirit-Empowered Living." It centers on discipleship in the 21st century with an emphasis on hearing God's voice. By the fall of 2016, the attendance in that class had soared to 746—this included students who enrolled from around the country and as far away as South Africa through what is called "simultaneous visual presence."

Notes Wilson, "With the help of technology they are able to see us in Tulsa, and we are able to see them and interact visually with them in distant locations."

At ORU, it seems that wherever you look, it's all about the "whole person"—the students.

A Spirit-Charged Atmosphere

While ORU makes headlines for its athletics, academics, and technology, what sets the university apart from every major educational institution is the dynamic, life-changing spiritual atmosphere.

Here's an example: A few years ago, a few students gathered together on Friday nights to pray for the university, their fellow classmates, and the nations. It has now blossomed into a huge, long-lasting spiritual awakening known as "Prayer Movement."

On weekdays, you'll find continuous, student-led prayer and worship taking place in the Prayer Tower auditorium from 4:30 in the afternoon to midnight—with students signing up for 90-minute slots.

Victor Mendoza, one of the coordinators, said, "I came here to be part of this, and I believe Prayer Movement is always going to be a central and key aspect of ORU's culture."

The campus Spiritual Formation Office is committed to assisting students by providing practical opportunities to operate in their giftings, grow in their faith, and fulfill their callings. This is accomplished through a number of avenues including missions, outreach, mentoring, worship, and prayer.

Each January there is a RenewU event—24 hours of focused prayer and worship, plus student ministers and open-mic testimonies. And when you attend an ORU chapel service and see the student participation, you will immediately know that this is a campus founded and focused on the Holy Spirit.

11

AHEAD OF THE CURVE

The quality of ORU's academic program has garnered the attention of corporations and major non-profits. This became evident when, in 2016, the National Science Foundation gave the university a $1.14 million grant through its Robert Noyce Teacher Scholarship Program—the largest ever received by the university.

It will provide funding for ORU's new Math and Science Scholarships for Teaching (MASST) program which addresses the shortage of science, technology, engineering, and mathematics (STEM) teachers within secondary, high-need schools.

During the five-year grant, the university's MASST program will partner with Broken Arrow Public Schools, Tulsa Public Schools, and the Tulsa Dream Center, providing specialized teaching internships to students. This hands-on experience will be of great benefit to ORU graduates planning to teach in these fields.

THE ONEOK SPORTS COMPLEX

The corporate world is also taking note. For example, the foundation of ONEOK, one of the nation's largest energy companies, based in Tulsa, provided the seed money for ORU's new state-of-the-art sports facility for track and field and tennis. Along with other designated gifts, it was built debt-free.

The groundbreaking ceremony was held during the university's 50th Anniversary Celebration and the facility is now complete.

This wasn't the first time ONEOK had invested in ORU. Four years earlier it gave a major gift to the university's College of Business toward building a technology boardroom, called the "Shark Tank"—modeled after the ABC-TV show which features celebrity business owners grilling prospective entrepreneurs. ORU's version allows students to have cutting-edge experience, pitching their ideas to investors around the world.

The ONEOK Sports Complex is the first outdoor track and field facility in the history of the university. In addition to a regulation 400-meter track, it has shot put, discus, javelin, high jump, and pole vault areas.

137

This new sports complex will allow student athletes the opportunity to take their skills and talents to the next level. They're able to train, practice, and compete with elite college programs across the country.

Track and Field Coach Joe Dial sees nothing but pluses for the complex, and comments, "Hosting future events for local high school and collegiate tournaments will ultimately increase ORU's fan base."

The new tennis facility will allow the scheduling of major tournaments and United States Tennis Association leagues. The ONEOK Sports Complex is projected to bring more than 15,000 visitors to campus each year.

THE GLOBAL LEARNING CENTER

Oral Roberts, a pioneer in using television to bring a Christian message to the world, built a production studio on the campus in 1977 where many of his "Prime Time Specials" featuring the World Action Singers were produced.

It was adjacent to the 11,000-plus seat Mabee Center. Since both round buildings featured the same style architecture, the television facility was nicknamed "Baby Mabee."

Over time, it became underutilized, primarily hosting

conferences and banquets. Then, as an outgrowth of Dr. Wilson's globalization vision for ORU, plans began to come into focus for a center on campus that would literally touch the planet. In 2014, the Board of Trustees approved the transformation of Baby Mabee into the Global Learning Center—and announced this during the 50th Anniversary Celebration.

Instead of a groundbreaking event, on March 25, 2015, board members, faculty, staff, and students participated in an official "wall-breaking" ceremony by taking sledge hammers to a designated wall on the west side of the building. At the event, President Wilson promised, "We are committed to making this one of the highest-technology facilities in higher education in Oklahoma and the surrounding states, and we believe God is going to help us do that." He added, "We are going to raise up leaders for the globalized world in the 21st century."

Two years later, after an $8 million-plus renovation, the vision became reality—or as some would say, "virtual reality."

The 54,000-square-foot center was paid for in full and is debt-free.

NOT YOUR MAMA'S CLASSROOM

Every aspect of the GLC is high-tech and far advanced

from what you would find on the average college campus. Let's begin with the classrooms:

- A Global Learning and Teleportation Classroom— Access in and out of the GLC to/from any and all continents. Quality of video conference moves people around the world at the speed of light (teleportation).
- A Studio Classroom—Studio for recording any style of distance education, instruction, or classroom media.
- A Virtual Reality Classroom—Full immersive virtual reality (VR) learning room (i.e., flight simulation, marine biology, engineering, etc.).
- A High Performance Computing Research Classroom—Global access when high performance computers are required.
- A Global Innovation Collaboration Classroom—The think tank for furthering the advancement of instruction.
- Distance Education Lab Classroom—Dedicated for classes online that require a lab or an experiential aspect.
- A classroom with portal augmented reality equipment that can be configured to help people with certain learning challenges.

- Faculty Excellence and Learning Classroom—A room
  to teach all online and traditional faculty on
  new technologies and innovative delivery methods.

These classrooms have advanced design, are multi-functional, and flexible. They are equipped with infrared 360-degree cameras on the wall that swivel to follow and record professors as they teach. The videos are available so students can watch the lectures if they miss a class or take classes from elsewhere.

Supporting the technology, the GLC has more than 60 wireless access points, internet connections from different service providers, and new switches to make sure everyone can access the learning resources they need.

Classrooms have touch technology, interactive SMART Boards, and other tools to give professors visually advanced options as they teach a wide variety of subjects. Classes and programs are recorded and stored on high-capacity file servers to be retrieved by students on their personal mobile devices or computers and by ORU satellite campuses worldwide. Plus, the professor and students in the classroom in Tulsa can see and hear the global students on video screens in the back of the classroom.

These global students can raise their hands, ask questions,

and participate in the discussion as if they were in the room.

The three-story building also includes a 750-seat multipurpose performing arts center, 13 offices, and a television production studio, Oklahoma's largest.

SWIMMING WITH THE DOLPHINS

GLC's third floor houses Virtual Reality and Augmented Reality labs offering students multidimensional, interactive experiences on any subject matter. This allows a person to not only learn from a book, or audio or video tape, but also in many ways to be engulfed in the material to a larger degree. President Wilson marvels at the learning environment: "It's three-dimensional. You might walk through a motor, or walk out onto the ledge of an oil rig, or take apart the human body and study it."

Here, students enjoy a multidimensional encounter that gives them the sense of being fully surrounded by the environment they are learning about—and they have access to more than 500,000 learning objects, from partial to full simulations in every industry.

Students don't just have one room on campus to experience augmented and virtual reality. Through an app on their smartphone, they can see images in 3D and manipulate them. More importantly, students no longer have to struggle to learn something only written on paper, and faculty can easily incorporate the visuals into their teaching by talking through what everyone's exploring.

Michael Mathews, ORU's Associate Vice President of Technology and Innovation, explains, "Culture is changing rapidly, and technology is a key catalyst."

Mathews points out that studies show how a student's capacity to learn is enhanced 300 to 400 percent in a virtual or augmented reality environment because it involves all the senses. He says, "What we're seeing is a revolution in learning, and in technology's effect on learning. Higher education will experience this first, but then it will go all the way down through K-12. Students will be acquiring knowledge in ways that were never thought possible. For those of us who are older, it sort of blows our mind, but for young people today, who have started with technology since they were two years old, learning how to operate their mom's smartphone, this is natural. It's just part of their life. So it feels second nature to them and will really enhance their capability to learn."

A GIANT LEAP FORWARD

When the plans for the Global Learning Center were

announced, it immediately caught the attention of those in Tulsa and the state, but it is now being acclaimed far and wide. Educators and innovators are flying in for a firsthand look, saying, "You're way ahead of the curve."

The university has received:

- The United States Distance Learning Association's Innovation Award.
- The Eduventures Innovation Award, designed to identify and honor higher education institutions that demonstrate significant innovations, including creative use of technology to boost student success.
- The 2017 Campus Technology Impact Award by *Campus Technology Magazine* for the virtual reality features of the GLC.
- The "Business Transformation 150 Award." In the fall of 2017, ORU's Michael Mathews was named to this elite list that recognizes the top global executives leading transformation efforts in their organizations. ORU was one of only four universities to be so honored.

One faculty member commented, "With the GLC, we now have the ability to take the best of ORU to the world and the best of the world to ORU."

In the words of President Wilson, "We are thrilled to be on the cutting edge of this technology, but more importantly, it is a giant leap forward in fulfilling our global mission."

For students at this innovative campus, tomorrow has arrived today!

12

LOOKING AHEAD

When the Five-Year Adaptive Plan was set into motion in 2015, it included a baseline, or a starting point from which tangible progress could be measured.

The reason it was named an "adaptive plan" rather than a "strategic plan" was so the University Planning Council and board could review the external factors and internal needs of the university annually. Says President Wilson, "Actually, we are engaging the review process a couple of times a year, so it's a very dynamic measuring tool for the future of ORU."

If there are adjustments needed or issues that must be addressed, they go back to the University Planning Council.

Two years into the plan, more than 115 key performance indicators were on target, and other objectives were added, such as a greater emphasis on the Hispanic community, a new graduation requirement that included an intercultural experience, and partnership with local churches in involving ORU students in world missions.

The year 2017 was celebrated for another reason: nine

straight years of rising enrollment, welcoming nearly 1,000 new students for the fall semester—the most ever at the university. All 50 states and over 100 nations were represented in the student population, up from 90 nations the previous year. Of significance is the fact that 84 percent of ORU freshmen returned from the previous year, the highest retention rate in recent history.

THE ONLINE EXPLOSION

The university's online and lifelong learning programs are also growing. Adults and non-traditional students can receive the same Whole Person Education that traditional students enjoy, but it is more accommodating to the working adult schedule, and undergraduate degrees can be earned in fewer than four years. The courses are taught by fully credentialed faculty.

ORU offers online bachelor's degrees in:

- Biblical Literature
- Business Administration
- Christian Caregiving and Counseling
- Communication
- Financial Management

- Human Resource Management
- Information Technology
- International Business and Ministry
- Leadership Studies
- Liberal Studies
- Management
- Marketing
- Ministry and Leadership
- Psychology

Plus, online students can receive the English Language Learning Certificate and Special Education Certificate. And registered nurses with an associate degree can earn their Bachelor of Science in Nursing (BSN) through ORU's 100% online RN to BSN program in as little as four semesters once prerequisites are met.

The university offers online master's degrees including Master's of Education: Curriculum and Instruction; Master's of Education: School Administration; and MBA in Leadership.

Once more, the university's commitment to excellence is being recognized. AffordableCollegesOnline.org ranked ORU's Theology and Communications degrees in the top 20 of their respective lists. And ORU's online Christian Counseling degree is rated number two by Best Online Christian Counseling Programs.

TOUCHING THE WORLD

Globalization has permeated the ORU experience—for students, faculty, and administration. Month after month there are international alliances being formed in business, education, athletics, missions, and more.

In May 2017, for instance, the university announced a partnership with Singapore-based Marketplace Leadership Institute, an international organization equipping business people with biblical principles of leadership.

At the cutting edge of preparing the whole person for the whole world is what takes place through ORU's Missions and Outreach office. This is where hundreds of students are linked with on-site organizations during spring break and summer.

In 2016, for example, ORU sent over 500 students on 50 teams in missions efforts in nearly 30 countries, including Uruguay, South Africa, Italy, Israel, and India. As a result, over 38,000 heard the Gospel and approximately 18,900 lives were practically impacted by team work projects.

One group headed to an orphanage in Ongole, India, where Jocelyn Swan, a senior Education major, helped conduct camps for 150 children each week. She described what a thrill it was to be Jesus with "skin on" to those kids.

The next summer, 2017, the ORU footprint was even larger and included teams in music, healing, and even soccer. Once more, it was life-changing for the students—and for those they encountered.

After graduating with the class of 2017, Haley Gray joined the student team headed for Japan. She describes being overwhelmed by the bright lights, the noise, and the thousands of people bustling around the sprawling city of Tokyo. During their first day of street ministry, Haley and team member Clare Holt really struggled to summon the courage to talk to anyone.

Then they met two high school girls named Aiko and Kyoka. After talking with them about their lives, the two ORU students shared the Gospel and gave their personal testimonies. Both Japanese girls accepted Christ, and after meeting up with them several more times, they were able to connect the high school coeds with a local Christian congregation. After returning home, Haley was thrilled to learn that the girls are still attending that church.

NEW HORIZONS

ORU's globalization effort took a significant step forward with the creation of the university's Office of Global Service. Named as Executive Director is Dr. Kevin Schneider from the College of Business, who has a stellar background in international finance. He is coordinating Study Abroad Programs, Healing Teams, and an Intercultural Experience for all graduates. He also oversees the International Student Center and Global Awareness Events on Campus, as well as Global Sensitivity.

Commenting on this appointment, ORU Provost Dr. Kathaleen Reid-Martinez said, "We already have international alumni impacting the world with God's healing. As our alumni base grows...we hope to establish collaborative access partnerships to develop learning communities on every continent. Dr. Schneider's international academic experience will allow us to do that."

Another appointment targets a specific culture. Dr. Eloy Nolivos was named as the University's Ambassador to Hispanic and Latin American Communities. The Ecuadorian native had been a member of the faculty, teaching Practical Theology. His work will center around building relationships and points of connectivity with Hispanic and Latin American educational institutions, churches, denominations, ministries, and parachurch groups for the purposes of developing synergistic educational partnerships and student recruitment on behalf of ORU.

Dr. Mike Rakes, author, educator, and pastor of Winston Salem First in North Carolina, who became Chair of the Board of Trustees in April 2017, comments, "I'm excited to be part of what's next at this great university as it continues training Spirit-empowered leaders through Whole Person Education."

WHAT ABOUT TOMORROW?

What does the future hold for ORU?

Dr. Wilson has given that question considerable thought and here are his observations:

From where I sit, the next 50 years at Oral Roberts University look amazing. Modern societies have shifted from being industrial-based to knowledge-based to, most recently, design-based. Within the next decade, many believe we will be living in an "intelligence-based society," accessing and utilizing information from every aspect of our lives.

Self-driving cars, automated medical attention, immersive entertainment, daily robotic assistance, and space habitation all have the potential of being commonplace in the years ahead. We will be living in the merging of all-things-digital and all-things-intelligent. Augmented and virtual reality will combine with machine language and artificial intelligence to create amazing new vistas of promise.

The days ahead are not for the faint of heart nor

for those who live in fear. New technological advancements will present unique challenges and new potential dangers for mankind. Yet we must face the future unafraid, believing that these new possibilities can be utilized for both the good of man and the advancement of Christ's kingdom in the world.

What do these amazing trends mean for education? Personally, I believe they mean endless opportunities, especially here at ORU. The convergence of information, technology, and intelligence will allow students to design their own college experience, from the coffee they drink, to the shoes they wear, to the advanced degrees they earn. ORU was the first university to have teleportation robots that beamed people into classrooms, and the first to import fitness data from wearable Fitbit watches into the grade book. We will continue to embrace and pioneer the full utilization of data and intelligence in our curriculum and in educating the 21st-century whole person.

From the moment it was founded, ORU has sped toward the future with open arms. It's the reason the university's administration fast-tracked accreditation. It's the reason we developed a sophisticated phone system that allowed students to dial into lectures long before such a thing might be commonplace. And it's the reason our faculty, students, and alumni are racing ahead to embrace new learning styles in our curriculum and in educating the 21st-century whole person.

ORU now has the potential to produce the most intelligent college graduates in the world, young men and women who wear and seamlessly use the technologies that are influencing every person's world today and tomorrow.

FINAL THOUGHTS

Dr. Wilson also looked ahead and envisioned the 100th graduating class and what things might be like at ORU in 2067:

- Will we be having multiple Commencement exercises each year at the Tulsa campus?
- Will we be holding ceremonies on different continents around the world?
- Might there be a student from every nation on Planet Earth graduating each year?
- Will all the students graduate by virtual presence in a virtual ceremony?
- How many new programs will we have?
- Has the Commencement speaker for the 2067 ORU graduation even been born yet?

- What new technological and educational advancements will we be using?
- Will our classes be taught by hologram?

President Wilson makes this final statement: "As exciting as the advancements are in this technologically intelligent future world, ORU remains committed to staying focused on its mission: to build Holy Spirit-empowered leaders through whole person education to impact the world with God's healing. In the future, the Holy Spirit will continue to be welcome at ORU, prayer will remain central, and God's voice will still be heard and obeyed by the greatest students in the world. Because what can be more futuristic than keeping our eyes focused on eternity?"

In conclusion, he adds, "It is impossible to anticipate all that the future holds for ORU, but as we reflect on God's blessings thus far, I believe we can proclaim with certainty that 'something good is going to happen' to this university in the years ahead."

EPILOGUE

In the introduction to *The New ORU,* we encouraged those both inside and outside the walls of the university to take the time to read this book because there is valuable knowledge to be gained and meaningful lessons to be learned.

What are these takeaways? Let us begin with the ORU family:

- **The Students**

  Their eyes have been opened to far more than the history and transformation of a remarkable university. They also have a better grasp of what it means to embrace a "Whole Person" education —that wellness is as important as the library, and social interactions with the community are greatly strengthened by their spiritual interactions with God in worship.

  Because of the increasing emphasis on globalization, their role in impacting the world presents endless possibilities and takes on an exciting new meaning.

- **The Faculty, Staff, and Administrators**

   Those in instruction, oversight, and support roles have acquired a deeper appreciation for presidential leadership and the necessity of working together as a team to achieve the goals of the vision for success in a high-tech world.

- **The Alumni**

   Former students can look in the rearview mirror of their lives and see the impact of ORU on their personal formation and development. And with the dramatic turnaround of the university in recent years, including the completion of Armand Hammer Alumni-Student Center, their loyalty and "pride of school" has increased and grown stronger.

- **The Donors**

   It has become clear that the financial backers of ORU have received a high return on their investment. They support graduates who are educated as *whole people*—not just individuals training for a career. From time to time, every stakeholder should re-read the forceful and eloquent commencement remarks of Jamie Weathers (in chapter 3) of why the world desperately needs the whole men and women that ORU produces.

FOR THE OUTSIDE WORLD

The ORU story also contains valuable insights for the trustees, faculty, and presidents of public and private universities. These include:

- **The Role of Vision**

    At Oral Roberts University, the founder had a clear statement of vision, which was later articulated in the school's mission. As we have seen, the vision *operationalizes* the mission.

    The members of the board have the responsibility of safeguarding the mission, and the president and faculty are responsible for translating that mission into a vision of success—the Five-Year Adaptive Plan being a case study for this.

- **The Role of Purpose**

    Purpose flows from vision, and it deals with "how we accomplish this." At ORU it involves the factors we have detailed, including financial enablement, scholarships, technology, and globalization.

- **The Role of Finances**

    An important goal of any educational enterprise

is mission fulfillment with economic sustainability. The board is responsible for both the short- and long-term financial stability of the institution—but we must never forget that it is driven by the mission.

• The Role of Governance

Finally, we tie these important cords together. Governance is a process that any university has to design, build, and maintain in order to balance the interests of the authority structures in the direction of mission fulfillment with economic sustainability.

We learned that governance is different than authority; it involves harmonizing the shared authority of the board, the president, and the faculty.

Regarding leadership, the president becomes the facilitator of the governance process.

Today, Oral Roberts University is a vibrant, Christ-centered, forward-thinking educational community. Tomorrow, its unchangeable vision and mission will continue to produce motivated students who are spiritually alive, intellectually alert, physically disciplined, socially adept, and professionally competent—who will, as the founder stated, "go to the uttermost bounds of the earth."

ORAL ROBERTS UNIVERSITY
7777 SOUTH LEWIS AVENUE
TULSA, OKLAHOMA 74171